THE HONORABLE WAY

THE HONORABLE WAY

by Edmonds Prufrock Mackey

STORY SCRIBE BOOKS

Kansas City   St. Louis

STORY SCRIBE BOOKS

Kansas City   St. Louis

A division of The Story Scribe
www.thestoryscribe.com
816-377-8694

Cover and layout design by Sarah Meiers

ISBN: 979-8-9863597-3-1 (Hardcover)
ISBN: 979-8-9863597-4-8 (Softcover)

Library of Congress Control Number: 2023945164

DISCLAIMER: This memoir is based on my own recollection of events, many long
past. They may not always be as others recall them. A few of the names of people
have been changed to avoid offense, including some place names. Any mistakes are
my own.

Except where noted, all poems were written by the author.

Printed in the United States of America

To Anne,
without whom this book
might never have been published.

In ancient Rome a young patrician passed
From his studies to the military and thence to public service.
This tradition was known as
Cursus Honorum,
The honorable way.

TABLE OF CONTENTS

The Sea

How shall I tell you of the sea?
Shall I tell you of dark nights
In still harbors,
Of sea gently blessing shore,
Quiet condescension of
Infinite to finite?
The luminous reflection of Man
Floats unnoticed on the ebb,
Confetti carelessly strewn,
An unconscious offering
Swept toward assimilation
In an uncertain eternity.

Shall I tell you of the timelessness
Beyond the land?
Blue days, black nights,
Gray, angry dawns?
Incessant count of
The immeasurable.
How shall I tell you of the sea
When none but fools
Would seek to 'compass time
Or fathom the Almighty?

San Diego, California Fleet Destroyer Base, 1962

USS Chevalier outbound

SO IT BEGINS

"We had the experience, but missed the meaning
And approach to the meaning
Restores the experience in a different form..."

– T.S. Eliot

My name is Edmonds Prufrock Mackey. I have three last names. With due respect to Mr. Eliot, the name Prufrock belonged to my family long before he wrote his poem. I was born into war and the last stage of the Great Depression. In March of 1939 Adolf Hitler's Blitzkrieg was driving into Czechoslovakia, a country which no longer exists. My life is my unique fingerprint on the page of time. I have been privileged to experience that time and places that are no longer and will never be again. I have no illusion or pretense that I am important. I merely hope to preserve some record of who I was for my family and for any who might seek to know something of my small place in time. I was to graduate from Princeton University in June of 1961, with little notion of what I might pursue. I would be armed with a degree from the History Department which did not seem to be the designation most valued by corporate recruiters.

Hamilton Hall, Princeton, April 1961

A few inches remained in the fifth, to which I had treated myself. My thesis was submitted. Its fate and mine were now in the hands of the reader. "The Significance of Nowhere." A suitably ironic title. The fifth and I had bottomed simultaneously. I was tired of writing and rewriting. I was tired of studying dead authors and dusty thoughts. Most of all, I was tired of the cynicism we ingested and sarcasm which we exuded to protect our male egos. I was tired of Princeton.

I exited Hamilton Hall with little pomp, and less circumstance. As I stepped into the courtyard, the sensuous warmth of the new spring filled the night and permeated my being. Magnolias in their full glory scented my way through Holder Court. I paused at the steps of Blair, with its Gothic arch and tower framing my escape. The star-splashed night settled about me a sense of hope and realization of freedom. In that moment, I felt the universe expanding and with it my consciousness. For an instant, I could understand and awe the vastness that is eternity. Humbled by the height of the heavens and the insignificance of my one small planet, I inhaled the night. It was once again spring in my minute corner of the Milky Way. I descended the steps, and upon reaching the bottom, I began to run. I ran as at the beginning of a race, with short, quick steps. Then, gaining speed, I lengthened my stride till I reached the P.J.&B. Station, spur to the Pennsylvania mainline. My timing was impeccable, if unconscious. I boarded just as the wheels began to turn toward the junction. The conductor retrieved my fare, and I settled into a seat by an open window. The odor of cow manure from the Princeton Dairy scented the night air.

NAVAL OFFICER CANDIDATE SCHOOL

NEWPORT, RHODE ISLAND

July 1961

"In accordance with authority contained in reference (a), you are directed to proceed in time to report to the Commanding Officer, U.S. Naval Schools Command, Newport, Rhode Island on 1 July 1961 for indoctrination, upon satisfactory completion of the prescribed period of indoctrination you will be appointed an Ensign, U.S. Naval Reserve with the General Line designator of 1105." BUPERS Orders

Punctuation had obviously not been the author's strong suit. Regardless of his infatuation with commas, I was signed up and sworn in. While my soul belonged to God, the rest of me was property of the United States Naval Reserve for the next three and a half years. I had enlisted. Though the golden bars of a commissioned officer gleamed in my future, their realization depended on my successful completion of the next five months as

ENS Edmonds P Mackey,
commissioned 17 November 1961

an OCSA, Officer Candidate Seaman Apprentice, the lowest life form on Codington Point, Rhode Island.

We were nine hundred who gathered to report to the Commanding Officer of the School's Command on the hot afternoon of 1 July 1961. We were here largely of our own volition. The assembly was predominantly Protestant and exclusively white. Most were graduates of the national college class of 1961. We were white, educated, and of some affluence, but were innocents in the ways of the military and of political purpose. We were about to be manipulated in the tradition of every sovereign nation that has called its youth to arms.

The mission of Naval OCS was simple. The U.S. Naval Academy and Naval ROTC could provide only half the Junior Officers necessary to staff the fleet. We reservists would provide the balance due. Ultimately the Annapolis alums would vie among themselves for the senior billets, while most reservists would muster out into the world of civilian commerce. Meanwhile those of us who survived OCS would swell the ranks as junior officers and man the lesser helms.

Had we been privy to the statistics, we might have wondered at being nine hundred rather than the normal seven hundred candidates. It seems the Navy was planning to be more occupied in Southeast Asia than was publicly published. Ultimately, a country called Vietnam would call certain of our numbers to unintended sacrifice.

This design was not readily apparent to those of us currently gathered on Codington Point in ill-fitting chambray, denim, and unshined boondocker boots. Had the intent been inscribed as an epitaph above the entry gate, it would have dissuaded few. As the Navy had its purpose, so had we our own. As long as nations and navies have manipulated youth, that long have young men sought the sea.

As for me, why did I sign up? There was the element of patriotism. I loved my country. I was a child of WWII. My cousins had served nobly. There was the love of history. The ancient Roman model of service intrigued me and seemed a noble path. The simplest answer was that I did not know what I wanted to be, but I did know what I wanted to do. I wanted to see the world. I had never been outside the continental USA, unless Niagara Falls counts. I had "joined the Navy to See the World," just as the WWII recruiting posters had promised. Anchors aweigh!

OCS was the military equivalent of Orwell's *1984*. Unlike the Marines' Parris Island, there was little physical conditioning. One just can't hike that far on the deck of a destroyer or even an aircraft carrier.

It was control and mind games, mine and theirs. Our world revolved about Alpha Avenue. It was lined with Korean-era "temporary" barracks for housing and classes. Along it we marched to the blare of martial marches in close formations from class to class or each time we left Charlie Company barracks as a section. For exercise, there were a few calisthenics and marching on the parade ground "grinder." But the games...

The game was Ensign or enlisted, Bars or bell bottoms. Fail the curriculum, "bilge out" in the vernacular, and you were sent to the fleet as a Seaman Apprentice. There you would sleep in tiered bunks with the ordinary seamen. There were only two types of enlisted at OCS, the Chief Petty Officer (sergeants of the Navy) who taught us, or the mess cooks who slopped gravy on our mess trays and could construct entire sentences from the principal parts of the work "fuck." The message was clear. Bilge out, and you sleep with the mess cooks.

Even our uniforms were a reminder of what might be if we bilged out. We wore bell bottom dungarees, chambray shirts, and white hats of the sailor. For liberty, if it ever came, we were permitted the summer Uniform of the Day, white bell bottoms, pullover blouse, and the distinctive white hat. Only if we successfully completed the first half of our schooling would we qualify to be issued OTUs, Officer Type Uniforms—the Dress Blue jacket and trousers of a commissioned officer.

The score was kept in "gigs," red or blue. Red Gig bad, Blue Gig good. 40 Reds and you bilged out, slept with the mess cooks in the fleet.

We marched in the dust of the parade grinder for two days before we were informed that we must be able to shave in the shine on our boondockers. We learned that "Irish Pennants" were not flags, but any tiny thread protruding from our chambray and denim. Each was gig-worthy at inspection. But the biggest chip in the game was the ENO, *Elements of Naval Operations*. A publication clearly marked **CONFIDENTIAL**. Basically this was a signal book for fleet maneuvers and operations. Possessed by every allied navy in the world and undoubtedly translated many times into Russian and Chinese. Loss of its possession was an automatic thirty gigs of one's forty. For the next five months, it must be either in hand or in locker. During that five-month period, we would ingest academically what the ROTC managed in four years of college. It took a 2.5 on a 4-point system to graduate.

A bit over a month ago, my evening slumber never began before 12:00 PM or 2400 in my new required vernacular. Reveille was 0530 hours in my new world. By 0600 I had "shit, showered and shaved," in the sailor slang. In addition, I had made my "rack" so tight a quarter would bounce from the sheet, squared away my locker and secured my "cleaning" station. By 0601 we were formed up and marching to the drum and bugle on a well-worn recording. In the mess hall, we would view our potential shipmates, the mess cooks, slopping slimy scrambled eggs onto our tin mess trays. Throughout the day, we marched from class to class without a break. The day finally ended at 2230. By which time, stripped to my skivvies, I dropped onto my rack. "Onto" being the operative preposition, as we all slept on top of the sheets to expedite the morning ritual.

We were introduced to a new vocabulary. Since many of us would be living on ships at sea, it was necessary that we speak the language of the sea…"Port," "Starboard," "Fore," "Aft," "Bow," "Stern." But this was no game. This was a matter of life, death, passing or collision. When the order was given, you had damn well better know how to answer your helm. But there was whimsy and tradition as well. A "scuttlebutt" was a drinking fountain. The term derived from the British sailors' propensity to gather near the freshwater cask or rum barrel to gossip. Scuttlebutt then was the ship's gossip or rumor. At OCS, the preferred form of this was the "gouge," solid information on what was to be contained in the day's test or actual test answers.

Never in my life had I been so controlled by a system, or so in control of my thoughts. There were no radios, televisions, or news-papers. There was no liberty during the first month. Even when it was eventually offered, I chose to remain on the base for EMI, extra military instruction, or "P-Works," extra practice in the art of celestial navigation and piloting. The focus of my thoughts was survival; to that end that there was no room for the outside world including the three "F's"—friends, family, or females. I literally would not allow myself any thought of the world outside OCS.

Our world was a series of rectangles. The space we inhabit is the rectangular second floor of a rectangular barracks. Perpendicular to the outside wall are our bunks. Two-tiered, upper and lower, which we seem to spend more time preparing for inspection than sleeping in. The space is divided in half by a row of gray metal lockers in which we keep uniforms, books, the few personal pos-sessions permitted, and our Garand Rifle. Perpendicular to the wall on the opposite side of the lockers are rectangular tables. In this area we study, shine boondockers, shine brass, joke, and bitch. It is a world of rectangles. It is a world reduced to tests and inspections. It is a world of scrupulous accountability. Those who manage the ardors of this rectangular world are known as "squared away."

To enhance my chance of survival and gain "brownie points," I joined the drill team. But that is a story for later...

So marched the days, as did we. Left, right, left...one foot before the other toward graduation or rollback. But there were special days, at least in the minds of our minders. Field Day. An opportunity to clean the barracks prior to inspection. One might be "Captain of the Head," "Colonel of the Urinal." Brass floor drains were shined as far down as an arm might reach. Inspectors searched for the smallest pubic hair. For a time my duty was a fire extinguisher. It was one of the ancient brass variety. Brass on brass with raised lettering. When handed to me, it looked like a relic not shined since the Spanish American conflict. I attacked with a "vigor" that would have made JFK proud. It gleamed, rather than just shining. It was my offering to the gods of OCS. Upon returning to the barracks following inspection, I found my triumph replaced...by a more tarnished ancient relic.

But as they tested and harassed us, we began to change. The disparate individuals who arrived on Codington Point began to come together as a Section, a Company, and a Battalion. To work as units and not individuals. We clipped on each other's Irish Pennants, squared away gig lines, and protected ENOS. One section leaving a test would pass the "gouge," test answers, to the next. "Cooperate and Graduate" was the cry. And of course, that was the point. No single individual drives a ship. It requires the efforts of well-trained teams manning stations and obeying orders without question. Literally a matter of life and death.

A ship? As a kid, I built model airplanes, not ships. P-38s and Mustangs, vintage WWII fighters. I had joined the Navy with no thought as to the vessel on which I might serve. On a bleak October morning as I marched down Alpha Avenue, it happened quite by accident. Between the rows of barracks, I caught sight of one of the few stretches of actual water visible to an OC. At that moment, a sleek vessel steamed into view. Her silhouette spoke of speed. Her gun mounts faced forward. She looked ready for a fight. Her sharp bow cut the water in a perfect white "V," she had a "bone in her teeth." She was the shape of freedom beyond the manipulation of OCS. She was a destroyer, and I was in love. I now had a goal that transcended mere survival. I would see the world from the bridge of a destroyer.

Living in groups intended to operate efficiently in battle did not preclude the necessity of proper hygiene and healthcare. In fact, it made the health of the individual one with the health and efficiency of the fighting unit. Military medicine was medicine en masse. Generally, we were treated as a Company. This meant being treated in groups of one hundred or more. The Doctor in charge was a Captain known as the "Head Pecker Checker," or old "Negative, Accelerate." We generally stood at attention buck naked in single line formations while he inspected our "short arms." Shots were administered with a type of air gun that shot a high pressure stream of vaccine directly into one's arm without the benefit of a needle. The downside to this procedure was that a slight flinch could cause the stream to cut a gash in one's arm.

Beyond military medicine, the Navy had a propensity to CIA (cover its ass) with records in one's service jacket. One of the most bizarre came under the heading of "DriveSafe." We as a battalion were seated in the gymnasium to view an epic film produced by the state of Ohio on the subject. It was titled *Death On the Highways*, an understatement. Basically it was thirty minutes of

Technicolor photos of vehicular mayhem which left blood and body parts strewn across the Buckeye State. The message was clear. DriveSafe. It was overkill, literally. Several OCs lost their lunch on their jumpers. No less than four fainted and were removed on stretchers. In a stroke of irony, within six months, one of my shipboard collateral duties was "DriveSafe Officer," doomed to show and view this masterpiece no less than fifty times.

Beyond the "mickey mouse" and manipulation was education. It was serious and intense, provided by fine and qualified instructors. The best of all were the CPOs, Chief Petty Officers. They were the Master Sergeants of the Navy with decades of experience. Our Company CPO was Harry, BMCM, Master Chief Boatswain's Mate, one of the survivors of the USS *Arizona* in Pearl Harbor.

Another was Marble, BMC. Rumored to have been reduced in rate, but sheltered from the ire of the USMC at OCS for having decked a Marine Second Lieutenant in Boston's "Combat Zone." Marble was, of course, from Marblehead Mass. He taught us Seamanship and more. Chief Marble was the quintessence of the Professional Navy. His forebears had stood before the mast on the Nantucket Whalers. He left his lobster fleet to serve his country at first word of Pearl Harbor. Marble's jaw was like the Maine Coastline, and his smile could have burned off a fog bank. On most days, his gray eyes twinkled as he rumbled "now gen'lemun, we are gonna talk about da wules uh da woad." But the day I remember, storm clouds crowded his brow. He was pissed. Not singularly, but terminally pissed. "Gen'lemun, you are not payn attention. Yr mickey mousing aroun. Just because this class is easier an celestial, don mean ya can offload it. The ocean's no joke. Most evry evolution can get a person hurt or kilt if summons not payn attnsun. This is not always gon a be a drill. Most of ya are gon ta end up officers, God luv ya. You're gonna be in the fleet and cause the Navy sez so, yur gonna give the orders. Ya know what they call the Carriers? Tin Can Openers. Carriers can cut a destroyer in half. I've seen a man's back broke, cause the wrong order dropped a motorwhaleboat out da davits on im. Gen'lemun, were talken spensive equipment an body parts. Bout four mons fum now, President Kennedy and congress gonna give ya a commission. That means that my thirty years gotta do what your six months says. You gen'lemun gonna have the conn an my ass, so I jus wanna make sure your payn attensun."

Marble's class was Seamanship, not Orientation, but he orientated us with words of hard experience no textbook could match.

The saying goes, "There are no atheists in a foxhole." OCS was right up there with foxholes. In my other life I was taught, "Fear of the Lord is the beginning of wisdom." I would like to think it was wisdom that brought me to Sunday Chapel, but I suspect it was mostly fear. I spent the better part of my five months at OCS in fear of failure. I spent the few weekends that might have been free, taking extra instruction. Sunday Chapel was my only respite from the relentless routine. My every thought and act had but one end, and that was not to "bilge out," or "rollback" to the Junior Battalion. My internal life and thoughts were as monitored and inspected as were my days. Memories were not permitted, and dreams of life beyond OCS were a frivolity I could not afford. Perhaps it was the aberration of a relaxed Sunday Routine that turned my steps to the chapel. It was located topside in one of the rectangles that housed the business of OCS. The room was simple but for the white-clad altar. Without crucifix, it might have been a civil courtroom with highly polished oaken benches. It soon filled with the white uniforms of the junior battalion interspersed with the coveted OTUs of the Senior Battalion. The sermon was based on Jonah and his prayer. "I prayed to the Lord in my distress, and he answered me..." I was in distress. I was in peril. I was in the belly of the whale. Was I Jonah? But chapel was a place of refuge. A place of momentary peace.

Sailor's Prayer

Oh, God of safe harbors,
Creator of storms and shoals,
Grant me the wisdom
To chart true my given course,
And the strength
To hold steady
My helm

Days passed. So did I, by the barest of margins. We were now the Senior Battalion, clad in OTUs for inspection. Graduation began to seem more than a distant glimmer.

We began to receive DOD (Department of Defense) forms for completion. Duty Station preferences. All my choices were destroyers. I wanted East Coast assignments, as they deployed to the Mediterranean, and I wanted to see Europe. I specified "no more Schools. Just send me to sea." I was naturally ordered to Fleet Gunnery School in San Diego, but I was to get my destroyer. Following Gun School, I was to report to the USS *Chevalier* (DD805), as Gunnery Officer. In a stroke of irony, I would be filling the post vacated by our Company Officer LTJG Murphy. CHEVALIER was currently undergoing refitting in Long Beach. Others received some surprises. One who thought he had opted for assignment in Argentina had misread his choices and was posted to Argentia, Newfoundland.

And remember the drill team? Drill teams from all sections of the graduating Battalion met in the gymnasium in which we had suffered through short arm inspections and DriveSafe. But now we were here to determine the "Best of the Best." Charlie Company, Section 3 Drill Team was composed of 12 disparate and possibly desperate men. Most had volunteered in hope of favorable treatment by the powers above. I was among them in spirit and also, since I had spent two years at a military prep school, was comfortable with close order drill. We were arranged by height, with the shortest in the front rank, right corner when viewed from astern, Karambelas. He was our GuideOn, from whom we took our alignment. "Dress right Dress." He also set the tempo of performance. With the Commanding Officer, OCS Staff, and Battalion gathered round, Karambelas spooked. He set off at twice the pace at which we had ever attempted our routine. We stepped out double time, as if marching on hot coals. By the time we knelt in our finale, the Queen Ann Salute, we were sweat soaked and shattered. Waiting for the final announcement from the judges, we were abject. The final decision from the judges was that the winner was unanimous, clear-cut, unambiguous...Charlie Company, Section 3. The keystone cops had accidentally pulled it off.

"I, Edmonds Mackey, do hereby accept the appointment as a Reserve Officer in the grade of Ensign in the United States Navy." Officers Oath.

Upon completion of our oath, 800 white officers' hats sailed into the air of the gymnasium. Not 900. Not all who began the race had finished.

As we filed out, we were each saluted by Chief Harry, BMCM, survivor of the USS *Arizona*, and in return, each handed him a silver dollar, the customary bounty for the first salute received by a commissioned officer from an enlisted sailor.

Unknown to the general public and without the consent of Congress, on 14 November 1961, President John Fitzgerald Kennedy determined to increase the U.S. presence in Vietnam from 1,000 to 16,000 "military advisors" over a two-year period. These facts were also unknown to the 800 graduates about to take their oaths of fealty and duty to the United States and assume the title of "Commissioned Officer."

In retrospect, 28 February 1961 would be decreed the beginning of the Vietnam Era.

On 17 November 1961 I was commissioned "Officer, Gentleman and Ensign in the United States Naval Reserve." My commission stated the Commander in Chief's confidence in my "Patriotism, Valor, Fidelity, and Abilities..." It was signed on behalf of John Fitzgerald Kennedy, President of the United States by John B. Connolly, Secretary of the Navy.

By the end of November, two years hence, John Fitzgerald Kennedy would be dead. John B. Connolly would be gravely wounded. I would be a Vietnam Veteran.

President of the United States of America.

To all who shall see these presents, greeting:

Know Ye, that reposing special Trust and Confidence in the Patriotism, Valor, Fidelity and Abilities of   EDMONDS PRUFROCK MACKEY   I do appoint him a Reserve Officer in the United States Navy in the grade of ENSIGN to rank from the SEVENTEENTH day of NOVEMBER, 1961. He is therefore carefully and diligently to discharge the duties of such office by doing and performing all manner of things thereunto belonging.

And I do strictly charge and require all Officers, Seamen and Marines under his Command to be obedient to his orders. And he is to observe and follow such orders and directions from time to time as he shall receive from me, or the future President of The United States of America, or his Superior Officer set over him, according to the Rules and Discipline of the Navy.

This Commission to continue in force during the pleasure of the President of the United States for the time being.

Done at the City of Washington this FIFTH day of SEPTEMBER in the year of our Lord One Thousand Nine Hundred and SIXTY-ONE and of the Independence of The United States of America the One Hundred and EIGHTY-SIXTH.

By the President:

828532

John B. Connally
Secretary of the Navy

PRINCETON REPRISE

19 November 1961
Princeton University Blair Tower Suite, 0100 hours.
One o'clock in the morning.

I am lying on the beer-stained sofa in my "civvies." I have been an Officer and Gentleman for nearly 48 hours. The khaki slacks and black Lacoste shirt are the clothing in which I arrived at Codington Point on 1 July. They have been neither worn nor laundered since taken into custody by the United States on that date. They are the only civilian clothes in my possession. The skivvies are Navy issue. By my side are two Valpac containing my entire military issue wardrobe for all service and seasons. They will move with me from duty to duty, ship to ship, ocean to ocean, for the next three years. For all intents and purposes, they contain all my worldly possessions.

It is a football weekend and the house parties are just getting into full revelry. Women at a men's college are always cause for celebration and inebriation. The parties proceed without me. I have a date of sorts, but she seems to have fallen in love while waiting for me to arrive. Six months ago, this might have seemed traitorous and a cause for belligerence, but it now feels inconsequential. Her interest is in Ben, one of my former roommates.

Ironically, Ben is to report to Newport and Codington Point on Monday. He will probably be hung over with a case of what he used to call the RGs. The Re Grets. Good luck, Ben. I outrank you. I do not envy him Newport in the winter where the ships make port with salt water frozen to the decks and rigging.

Everything here is gray or snow-covered. There is something of the surreal. I am here, but not really. The cynicism and sarcasm of June have been supplanted by a sense of purpose and promise. This is someone else's world now, and they are welcome to it. The sky is still high and the world wide. And I am about to take its measure. By Monday, I will be in Kansas City for Thanksgiving. By 1 December, I will be in San Diego on USS *Shields* (DD596) for temporary assignment until Gunnery School in March. I will be, as the song says, "Out there having fun, in the warm California sun."

Anchors aweigh.

UNDERWAY

Deck Log Book USS Chevalier (DD805)
Saturday 18 May 1963
000-0400

Moored in a nest of 5 ships with standard mooring lines doubled. Ships from port to starboard are the USS Wiltsie (DD716), USS Chevalier (DD805), USS Marshall (DD676), USS Boyd (DD544) and USS Prairie (AD 15), with USS Prairie moored fore and aft to Buoys 28 and 29 in San Diego Harbor. Ships present include various units of the U.S. Pacific Fleet, foreign men-of-war, merchantmen and district craft.

Signed,
E.P. MACKEY, OOD
LTJG USNR

The destroyer tender, PRAIRIE, is moored fore and aft to buoys in the harbor, a few hundred yards from the Broadway Pier. CHEVALIER and her sisters are attached side by side to the mothership like ducklings. Each ship is connected one to another and thence to PRAIRIE by umbilicals through which they draw the water and electricity sustaining them.

In the hours before departure, CHEVY and her sisters will be born anew. Each vessel will assume a life independent of the land and one another. Boilers will be lighted and generators will begin to exhale their giant hum. Evaporators will commence distilling fresh water from the sea to provide steam for the turbines and life for the crews. With their holds full of stores and bunkers topped off with oil, the division can subsist for a week at sea without refueling or replenishing.

CHEVY, herself, is as long as a football field and a little wider at the waist than the depth of the end zone. While reluctant to disclose a woman's weight, records show that fully provisioned, she displaces 2250 tons of seawater. With a top speed of 32 knots, she is one of the smallest, fastest ships of war in the U.S. Pacific fleet. She is the womb of life in which her 180 enlisted men and 20 officers will dare the vast Pacific.

As the log attests, I am now a Lieutenant Junior Grade (LTJG). With most of the officers of my date of rank and following completion of eighteen months service, those of us who have not run a ship aground nor insulted the Fleet Admiral, stand promoted. In my case, those months as an Ensign were more productive and educational than any in my life to date.

Naturally, BUPERS assigned me to Fleet Gunnery School in San Diego and thereafter to a West Coast destroyer, currently being rebuilt in a Long Beach shipyard. It seems BUPERS knows best. I love Southern California and the CHEVALIER. During the past eighteen months, the thing I wanted most was to be competent, to be "salty." To be worthy of the commission I had been granted. But experience must be earned, it cannot be bestowed. The price in this case was eighteen months. Here's to you, Chief Marble!

The eagle and gold braid on my Officer's hat now have a sufficient tinge of salt corrosion to declare me "seasoned" to the new

Ensigns of the fleet and slightly less suspect to the Chief Petty Officers. I have earned my new half stripe.

The Deck Log further attests that I, as a bachelor officer, have drawn the Midwatch. The married Officers are bidding a seven-month farewell to wives and loved ones. Bachelor officers will be discovering new loved ones in WESTPAC.

The last few weeks have been frenetic, with service craft delivering last-minute provisions and supplies. For now the watch and the night are quiet, trending toward peace. Marks, my Petty Officer of the watch, and Steckel, my messenger, are fighting boredom by field stripping the Colt .45 sidearm required to be carried by the Petty Officer of the watch. The sidearm is mostly ceremonial and is not loaded. But then, who would attempt to attack a U.S. Warship in port?

I don't anticipate much activity. The most predictable event would be the Shore Patrol returning a sailor from an over-celebrated liberty. I take a walk to inspect the topside spaces, but mostly to absorb the scene of my last night in the U.S. for seven months. I take the moment to view office buildings of the city, silent sentinels of downtown. The lights of the skyline are reflected like luminous confetti on the ripples of the harbor. I inhale the night and with it the promise of tomorrow and the Orient.

Saturday 18 MAY 1963 0800

Mustered the crew at quarters. 0815 Stationed the special sea detail. 0845 completed all preparations for getting underway. 0911 Underway for Pearl Harbor, Hawaii LTJG BIDDLE at the conn, Captain and Navigator on the bridge. 0922 Maneuvering at various courses and speeds to clear the harbor. Deck Log

We depart with a flourish. On the deck of PRAIRIE, flags are flying and a Navy Band is playing "Anchors Aweigh." Clustered on the main deck of PRAIRIE, the brave smiles and tears of the gathered dependents bid "Godspeed." We go forth to enforce our nation's interests in the Far East as our leaders may see fit to demand.

I am stationed with my Division on the foc'sle for Sea detail. We stand in formation facing the bow, forward, hands clasped behind our backs at "parade rest." The detail is not ceremonial. We are prepared to man the lines or capstan on any orders from the bridge. Wilbur, Bo'sun mate 1, is on the sound powered phones to the bridge two decks above. I can see Doug Biddle, OOD on the port wing of the bridge waiting for WILTSIE to clear our mooring. Captain and XO are up there as well, hidden by the reflection from the pilot house window. When the last line has been cast off, a gentle ebb tide and a light breeze move us away from the nest, setting us to port. A conning officer's dream, as nature herself is drifting us away from MARSHALL and the nest. Doug orders "both engines ahead one third," and sounds one long blast on the ship's horn to signal that we are "Underway"—underway for Pearl Harbor, one week away, and then on to WESTPAC, the Western Pacific 4000 miles around the globe.

We maneuver out the channel dogging WILTSIE, 500 yards ahead and followed by MARSHALL astern. One by one, the members of Task Group 19.1 fall in line as we stand out of San Diego harbor. The tender, PRAIRIE, the dependents, and the Broadway Pier fall slowly away as we increase forward momentum. We split the paths of the Coronado Ferries as they scissor from city to island and back.

It is a postcard day for the Chamber of Commerce. The light morning fog has been banished by the warm sun of mid-May. The mountains to the east are actually visible for the first time this year. The breeze is light and the day warm as we maneuver out of the channel, passing the cruiser, *Saint Paul*, and the other moored craft of the U.S. Pacific Fleet. We pass the La Playa fuel pier to starboard and head toward Point Loma.

Port, Starboard, Odd, Even, Red and Green. The channel markers we pass are shaded and numbered with intent. They are the measure of the harbor and the last "fare thee well." They mark the safe track home or the path to the limitless deep. The mottled browns and greens of Point Loma fall astern to starboard. We bisect the wake of WILTSIE as it fans before our bow, joining ours to vanish in an ever-widening "v." We are abreast of channel buoy 1 SD, the last channel marker east of Pearl Harbor, one week away.

As we clear the channel, with our huge brass propellers churning, we catch the first swells of Open Ocean, surging forward into history and backwards in time. Soon we will be beyond the limits of electronic navigation. We enter God's ocean in much the same manner as did the mariners of the mid-1700s. Fixing our location in an ocean that covers two-thirds of the globe will depend upon the sextant. Fortunately, those taking celestial sightings through the sextant are more adept than I. The rub. Should the heavens be obscured means one is S.O.L. "Surely out of luck." Our path becomes a guess called "Dead Reckoning," An unfortunate term. The "Dead" does not inspire confidence, as one is forced to apply speed and course changes to a chart without benefit of the corrections for the battering of wind, sea state, and current. The longer one is without stars, the more "dead" the reckoning. S.O.L. As we sail on, the grays of the harbor fade, and the ocean glistens with an ever intensifying blue. CHEVALIER is now a small world in a mighty sea, dependent upon the collective skills of her officers and crew to survive.

Now, clear of the harbor, we are fighting ships, and it is time to take up the business of defense. The Task Group Commander orders a protective circular screen formed around his command ship, the Guided Missile Destroyer, TOWERS. So we nine "cowboys" scramble to our designated places and ride herd. From the bridge of towers, perhaps the Commodore feels a moment of pride and power as he orders his command forward. The lone gull far above sees only a circle of gray dots arranged about a slightly larger dot. In the Pacific, great men and ships grow small.

CHEVALIER is a "man-of-war" and "armed to the teeth." For our ASW, anti-submarine role, we carry the latest electronic homing torpedoes, no longer the depth charges of WWII. We carry the latest sonar system for sub detection mounted beneath our bow. For anti-aircraft, anti-ship, and shore bombardment, we have three twin-barreled 5"/38 gun mounts. They are mine. As a gunnery officer, I shoot the guns. A boy's dream. My bullets weigh 58 pounds and can travel ten nautical miles. When I fire a broadside, the ship is physically set sideways in the water.

As we cleared the harbor, the CO ordered the crew exercised at General Quarters. We assumed our positions from which we would "fight" our ship. For that reason, I am currently seated in the Main Battery Director, the position from which I fire the guns. The Director sits one level above the bridge and just aft. It is the best seat in the house. It is the highest position on the CHEVY other than the masts and the two stacks. It is my favorite spot on the ship. From here I can survey the bridge and the entire forward part of the ship to the horizon. Not to enjoy myself but to better spot the enemy. But I enjoy myself anyway. What a toy. The director itself is a metal box with a radar dish atop. At battle stations, it contains a crew of four. I sit on a high metal seat that projects me chest high through a hatch. The effect is not unlike that of a tank commander. Before me is a set of binoculars attached to a hand control with which I can slew the director. My role is to acquire the targets that the guns shoot. I look through binoculars to acquire the ship or aircraft target. Once I have the target in my sights, the radar operator will "lock" the radar on to the target and we will continue to "track the target in automatic." The radar then sends a signal to an analog computer in the bowels of the ship, which calculates a firing solution. The gun mounts are then synchronized with the solution and I await the CO's order to release the guns and commence firing. A trip, so long as all I have to shoot is targets, and not real people. Thank God, I will never have to fire guns in anger.

Buoy 1 SD

The Bell Buoy bobs and floats alone,
A truncated sentinel,
Of
Departures and returns.
The land, low on the horizon,
Emerges and vanishes from view,
At the whim of the undulant sea.
There it might remain,
Survivor of the nuclear maelstrom,
Clanging
Into the stillness of an eternity
Without Man.

The CO orders our course due west, 270, and we secure from General Quarters. I order the guns trained centerline and secured. Tompions will be inserted in the barrels to protect the interior rifling from sea water. Those of the gun crews not on watch will return to their day jobs. The watches, crews of men necessary to sail the ship 24 hours a day, rotate in four segments. But we all have our day jobs as well. There is no boredom on the sailing man's seven day ocean.

I steal a few minutes for myself in the director to watch the last buoy west of Pearl Harbor vanish astern below the horizon. Here I sit, a khaki-clad Jonah, shaded by the circular fire-control radar dish. We are embarked.

A WEEK AT SEA

Saturday, 18 May - Friday, 24 May 1963

While we were still in the yards in Long Beach, my aunt and uncle docked on the ORIANIA, the cruise ship upon which they just sailed the Orient. I traded them a tour of Disneyland for a meal on the British ship. The meal itself began with cocktails and proceeded through at least five courses, finishing with savories, cheese, and brandy. By this time, about 10:00 P.M., there was a late supper being prepared on the upper deck, should any traveler be the least bit peckish. During supper, the cruise directress paused to ask after our comfort. "My biggest challenge is keeping our passengers busy. We have entertainment, lessons, exercise, and bridge. How do you possibly keep your crew from being bored for a week at sea?"

The sailing man's seven-day ocean. At 0800 we mustered the entire crew at quarters. By this time they would have made their racks, squared away their lockers and quarters, and had chow. All officers and men not on watch fell into formation at the place on the ship assigned to their division. There they were counted, inspected, and given their orders for that day. The officers then fell into a separate formation to be inspected and receive orders from the XO. Department heads met with their junior officers to pass the word. For those who had the Morning Watch, the 0400 to 0800, tough. Their day began at 0400, tough. If we happened to have an "all hands" evolution before the morning watch, tough. One could be up for days during fleet operations. We all had day jobs. The ways of the sea are relentless. As the sea never sleeps, sometimes nor do we.

A ship's world is governed by "Watches," the incessant division of hours at sea. Each watch is four hours, with the exception of the "dog" watches, the 1600 to 1800 and the 1800 to 2000. The Dog Watches allow the crew to eat the evening meal, as 1800 is 6:00 PM. The break also creates the rotation so that each watch section rotates forward to the next watch daily.

What happens during a week at sea? If we are operating with an Aircraft Carrier in the war zone, much. If we are simply in transit, we practice for the business of war and survival in an ocean whose breadth and depth and power defy imagination. We are currently about the business of "getting there," which fills each day with the challenges of the sea.

We have begun to practice survival.

Division Nest departing for WestPac

Wednesday 22 MAY 1963

1245 Exercise the crew at General Quarters. Set condition 1AA, set condition ZEBRA. 1325 commenced firing. 1350 ceased firing. 1352 maneuvering to recover target drone. Deck Log

As we near Pearl Harbor, I am back at my battle station in the Main Battery Director. Condition 1 AA presumes an air attack is imminent. Condition ZEBRA secures all watertight passages and hatches to reduce flooding from battle damage. Most of our condition 1AA drills simply involve timing the crews' reaction time until "manned and ready." Reaction time is survival. Today we have secured a practice drone aircraft to act as a target for our 1AA 5" guns. If we were in actual combat, my team FTs and Gunners' Mates and their comrades in the gun mounts would be a team responsible for shooting the attackers from the skies. An offset is applied to the firing solution to prevent damage to an expensive drone, but the powder and projectiles are real. One of my day jobs.

But we have no known enemies in this part of the globe, so 1AA is preparation for a future contingency in WESTPAC. Most of our drills are more pragmatic and presume the possible.

The cry of "Man Overboard..." "Port" or "Starboard" may be issued at any time of the day or night, hopefully followed by the advice "this is a drill." Immediately the Conning Officer must order the helmsman to put his helm in the proper direction to execute a "Williamson Turn," a maneuver calculated to reverse the ship's course on the exact track it was following at the cry. One of my Gunners' Mates had been a man overboard, unnoticed. His cries unheard. He said it is the most lonesome feeling in the world to see the masts of your ship disappear below the horizon while you float in the deep unnoticed and unheard. Fortunately, the ensuing search recovered him.

Drills for "Steering Casualty," "Binnacle Compass Failure," and "Engine Failure" along with fire and damage control were added to our list of drills for which OOD and crews must be prepared.

Chief Marble's exhortation, "Gn'l mun, pay attensun. We're taken expensive equipment an body parts..." was sinking in.

So the drills have their purpose beyond the obvious, as it did the drills at OCS. They bring us together as a team, a crew bent on survival in war or peace on the naked edge of the world.

The Navy and its branch, the Marine Corps, are volunteer services. None of our men have been drafted. Each has volunteered for his own purposes. Each of our 180 men plays a specific role or roles in the manning and defense of our vessel. There is a direct, specific order of responsibility that passes from the Commanding Officer, through the Executive Officer, the department heads, and down to the lowliest Seaman Apprentice. The commanding officer of a ship at sea is an absolute monarch, with the power of life and death over his command. As such, he is also absolutely responsible for the ship, its action, and that of his crew.

Our C.O. is John Stanko, CMDR, USN. He is called "Captain," as is any man who commands a commissioned Naval ship, regardless of rank. Upon expedited graduation from the U.S. Naval Academy in 1943, he was assigned to the submarine USS TARPON (SS 175). Captain Stanko served the entire war as a member of that sub crew in the Pacific Theater...and survived. The dark circles never seem to leave his countenance, which tends to make him look like a masked bulldog with jowls. He is a firm and fair leader of men, but has a good sense of humor and a tendency to hold conservative opinions on a variety of subjects. He has daughters, ages 7 and 8, and a wife, "Chick," who calls him "Stinky." During this deployment, his Annapolis class will become eligible for promotion and a fourth gold stripe. He is on the bridge as we begin our approach into Pearl Harbor. We have transited roughly the distance from New York to London. We have crossed about a third of the Pacific on our way to Japan.

HAWAII

Friday, 24 May 1963

We have been able to see the echoes of the Hawaiian coastline on our radar for some hours. Now the black and green volcanic peaks have begun to sprout above the distant horizon, as they once cataclysmically emerged from the sea itself. A land before man. Nothing but the volcanic core of the islands is domestic. Their fabric is largely the product of nature's flotsam and jetsam. The winds and currents made their periodic deposits from the reaches of the Pacific and the seabirds shat seeds upon the land. Erosion, sun, and rain did the rest, transforming the black lava into paradise.

But the crew of CHEVALIER would settle for less than paradise after nearly a week at sea. While we have been underway, there has been no news of the world beyond our bulkheads. Warships do not chatter. What information passes between and among ships is operational and in coded sound bites. Any further information of a more serious nature is sent in code and mechanically decoded in the "crypto" center. Its dissemination is tightly controlled and disseminated on a strict "need to know " basis. There always seems to be scuttlebutt, but even that has been sparse and uninteresting. Weather and time permitting, there might be a crew movie on the hangar deck. Other than books, one must keep one's own counsel and sleep when possible. It is difficult to imagine the plight of the windjammer seamen, at sea for months and years on end. Wooden ships. Iron men.

Our Task Group is now a line of ships playing follow the leader into Pearl Harbor. It is 0730 when we pass the first channel marker west of San Diego. The sun is just becoming visible between the twin peaks that frame the moorings. It is between those peaks twenty-two years ago on a Sunday morning that the first Japanese Zeros screamed like maddened hornets to wreak havoc. They came in low, barely clearing the landmass, with the rising sun at their backs and with villainous intent. They left behind a phantasm of smoke and flame, of twisted steel and splattered blood. They left the fleet in shambles and American interests in the Pacific defenseless. Unfortunately for Yamamoto, he missed the fuel bunkers, dry docks, and the carriers. In doing so, he lost the war.

I could imagine Chief Harry, then an ordinary seaman who had chosen to sleep in the cool of the open deck, shaking his head in disbelief at the foreign wing markings and Asian faces. Family legend has it that my great aunt Catherine manned the machine gun of a fallen soldier during the attack.

We follow the channel past the scars of history. The ghosts of Pearl Harbor. As we pass Ford Island, "Battleship Row," to port, the banks are lined with old 16" gun barrels, arranged as if for burial, nearly blanketed with vegetation. Nature taking back its own. The huge cement moorings of the capital ships are crowned with weeds. But the spirits of men lost and ships savaged linger. The water of the channel is still befouled with oil that seeps as tears from bunkers of ships dead these many years.

While most moorings are empty, one is not. Astride the remains of the USS ARIZONA, seemingly afloat, is a huge white rectangle with concave top. Completed the previous year, it was conceived to replicate the bridge from agony to victory in the Pacific conflict. Shrine to over a thousand men who lost their lives on that Sunday of devastation and who remain below, buried beneath the rusted stacks and rigging of their murdered vessel. There is a respectful silence and barely a breath among my men on the foc'sle as we make the turn to approach our mooring.

0906 Moored starboard side to USS TOWERS (DD 9) at berth B-25 in a nest of two destroyers, US NAVAL STATION, Pearl Harbor.

Side by side, we are an aged David and modern Goliath. Though nominally a destroyer, TOWERS is nearly the size of a cruiser from the last war. We are refurbished WWII. She is a Guided Missile Frigate, the latest offering from Bath, Maine.

Our business in Hawaii is replenishment. We are taking on fuel and groceries for the next leg of our voyage. We are also off-loading a restless crew for "R&R." Captain Stanko reminds the crew that "R&R" stands for Rest and Recuperation, not Rape and Rampage. I intend to be "on the beach" with them as soon as I am granted permission to take shore leave by the department head. It will be my first step onto land not contiguous with the continental US. Mahalo Hawaii.

I might have been fully focused on the prospect of exploring Oahu, were it not for a problem of some delicacy. Since departing San Diego, my left testicle had slowly increased to the size of a handball. While our corpsman, Smith, was a master of hangovers, this inconvenience was well beyond his APC and "green dragon" therapy. I am on my way to Tripler Army Medical Center and a certified "Pecker Checker." In the upper reaches of the island, I arrive at a massive aggregation of vertical and horizontal pink rectangles variously arranged against a backdrop of lush hills. A flamingo pink hospital? I can guess what General Patton might have called it.

Many of the military doctors come directly from residency. They trade eight years of service for med school tuition. Upon graduation, in the Navy, they receive the two silver bars of a Full Lieutenant. Unfortunately, they are given so little military indoctrination that they are likely to salute a Boy Scout, if they remember to salute at all. Mine fits the pattern but was competent and sympathetic.

"Epididymitis. Non-specific Urethritis. Any ideas how?"

"No women, sadly. I did drink a beer at the Bullfights in Tijuana a couple weeks ago."

"It is called 'non-specific' because we're not always sure how you get it. It's not VD. But it can cause sterility. I'm going to ship you back to the states."

"No!"

"What do you mean, "No?"

"That means no sir, no way, no how! Give me a shot of penicillin and clear me. I traded four years of my life to see WESTPAC, and that is where I am going!"

"I don't advise it. You will have to sign a release."

"I'll sign in blood, yours or mine? Where's the form?"

And then I am on my way to see Oahu, with Flamingo Stonehenge in my rearview mirror.

EN ROUTE TO
MIDWAY ISLAND

Monday, 27 May 1963

0835 Underway for Midway Island as a unit of Task Group 19.1. Maneuvering at various courses and speeds standing out of Pearl Harbor. 0850 Passed Buoy 1 to starboard.

We will not pass this buoy again until late November. For now, we are outward bound as CHEVALIER and her crew are caught up by the first swell of the open sea and embraced by the rhythm of the deep. Today the waves have a slow sensual motion that seems to welcome our hull and caress it. But the sea has many moods, and we will see them all before our journey's end.

It is 1500, and both Dick Hart and I are together in our shared living quarters, "Forward Officers." This is somewhat unusual as we are in different duty sections. I stand my watches on the bridge as a conning officer, and Dick in CIC, the Combat Information Center aft of the bridge. We are both a bit sunburned and hung over following our quest for the perfect Mai Tai on Oahu.

This is our refuge. Just the two of us, whereas all the other officers, including the XO, live in "After Officers." Only the CO has his private cabin. But privacy comes at a price on a destroyer. We are not air conditioned, and there are no portholes below the waterline.

Forward Officers is located just forward of the Wardroom and one deck below, starboard side. In wartime we might as well have a bull's eye painted on the hull beside our bunks. We are in the largest part of the CHEVALIER'S silhouette, just below the bridge and directly aft of the powder magazines for Gun Mounts 51 and 52.

Other than the lack of A/C, there is the matter of movement. The most stable section of a ship at sea is the center of its length. The mechanics are something like a see saw, with bow and stern moving up and down with wave action. A vessel is moved by the sea in three separate ways, pitch, yaw, and roll. Pitch is the vertical seesaw motion, roll is a rocking side by side. Yaw is a horizontal side to side motion of the stern like an exotic dancer shaking her buttocks. At sea, these movements become a series of synchronous motions. Sometimes subtle, but often inconvenient.

On my last ship, my bunk was built against the bulkhead without a frame. In heavy seas, I would actually roll up the bulkhead and back into my bunk. On CHEVY, I sleep in the upper bunk, which is surrounded by a 12-inch frame, preventing my bulkhead excursions. Originally, this accommodation had both a mattress and springs. I discovered during shakedown that the springs were impractical. When a ship pitches, the bow moves violently upward as it strikes a wave, then drops like a cable-less elevator into the trough. The further forward on a vessel, the more drastic the drop. The effect of this action on my springs was dramatic. As the ship rose on a wave, the springs compressed. The plummet into the trough released the springs, flinging me into orbit.

Upon return to port, I had Urbano banish my springs, I cared not where. I now sleep in a rectangular box atop my mattress. By sleeping on my stomach with my right knee cocked outward for balance, I negate roll and yaw as well. I have mastered the art of sleeping in Forward Officers.

For Dick and me, FO is our womb at sea. Our private domain. I do not believe any officer has ever entered our space. In fact, it is entered only by steward's mates who make our racks and the messenger of the watch to wake us.

Dick constructs electronics from his Heath kits, and I bang away on my Olivetti.

My rack is my refuge. Here I read and write. I place my hand on the steel bulkhead and feel the vastness of the Pacific slide past, mere inches from my fingertips.

MIDWAY

Thursday, 30 May 1963

1058 Steering various courses and speeds to go alongside Pier 2, Midway Island.

Technically, Midway Islands. There are two. Sand Island, to which we are currently attached, and Eastern Island, home to the abandoned Marine airstrip. We have transited over a thousand nautical miles since Pearl Harbor and are approximately another thousand plus miles from Japan.

Midway is a speck so small that no scale employed to illustrate it on a chart is sufficiently insufficient. Technically, the pin prick is a coral atoll composed of two lumps of sand and an iguana-like string of shoals, all perched atop an ancient volcano. The largest lump, about one square mile, is Sand Island. First discovered by an American sea captain in the mid-1860s, its only significance is location. It is roughly midway between Hawaii and Japan. An ideal fueling and replenishment stop. The first President Roosevelt declared it a "naval reservation" in 1903. Since then it has been inhabited mainly by US Marines and goony birds. The birds presumably were there first. While Marines are Marines, the Goonies are worth reflection.

The Laysan Albatross, better known as "Goony," is perfectly named. They appear much like a super seagull with large, webbed feet. On land, they lack the swagger of the smaller gulls. They are remarkable, if for nothing else, their sheer numbers. They are everywhere. They dot the land and clog the runways. The island is flat and barely above sea level. The highest point is clearly a palm tree with a Goony perched atop. To my right, a local inhabitant is cutting his lawn with a power mower. He swerves to avoid the bird, leaving the swath uncut and the Goony unmoved. They seem aware of their protected status and are, as it were, unflappable. The young are the size of a fluffy bowling ball, balanced on too-large feet, with a great hooked bill protruding from the top. To watch an adult attempt flight is nature's joke. They are forced to run into the wind with wings wide spread to gain sufficient lift for their bulk. Once airborne, they soar and gyre with the most graceful of gulls...but then to land...their bulk is such that they seem unable to light. Again they are forced to run, but with stubby legs to match the speed of descent, they tumble tail over beak in a disheveled pile of feathers.

The sky and lagoon are complementary blues, with a slice of palm and sand between. We stop at the officers' club in search of the last cold beer east of Japan, but find it tepid. Even refrigeration is challenged here, so we move on.

We walk until we find the plaque. In memoriam. Twenty-two years ago, Midway secured its place in history. If Pearl Harbor was the Yin, then seven months later, Midway proved the Yang. From the island, the shapes of rusting sunken hulks are still visible, though many lie in the much deeper graves beyond the reef. Unlike Pearl Harbor, the bones commemorate an American victory. They speak of sacrifice and valor, not shame. The bronze proclaims the day and the deed, but few will mark the spot.

Perhaps the irony was lost on Admiral Yamamoto, but likely not. He was a smart man and acted on orders contrary to his martial instinct. On June 4, 1942 his armada of one hundred and eighty ships approached from the north. From above, his force must have seemed like gray paint splatters on the Pacific blue. He believed he was setting a trap for the carriers he missed at Pearl Harbor. But fate, the Pacific, and a broken code betrayed him as he became the hunted and Nimitz forces the aggressors. Even so, detection by the Japanese caused Nimitz to launch his first strike much earlier than planned. His first wave of pilots left their carrier knowing that their fuel was insufficient to return. The battle raged four bloody days. Two giants bashing one another from afar. A battle in which the surface combatants never saw one another as death rained from the skies. Midway served notice that air power would determine the war's outcome, and that would be Japan's surrender. The Japanese navy was dealt a mortal blow at Midway, but there was much more dying to do. Who rules the air ultimately rules the sea and then the nation.

But at what price
Do navies wrest the rule
Of air and sea?
It was a day
When Death laughed with glee
To be fed brave pilots
Of both sides
So carelessly.

THE ORDER OF
THE GOLDEN DRAGON

Small gray ships
On a
Mighty sea
Cherished
for their
audacity

1 June 1963

O ur modest armada steams west north west, from Midway into the uncharted reaches of the Pacific. We are encompassed by naught but sea and sky in a vastness that stuns the senses. The horizon and sea seem to blend. Perhaps we are but figures in God's snow globe, to be shaken at his displeasure. Our next landfall is 900 nautical miles to the west.

But wait, what has happened? We seem to have misplaced a day. How careless of us. What happened to May 31? It seems to be missing from the log as well. Where does time go when you lose it?

30 May 2000 to 2400. 2359 Set all clocks ahead 24 hours to conform to the time zone - 12(M). Date advanced to 1 June 1963.

We have crossed the International Date Line. We have met the sun moving west and passed into tomorrow. Have I been shortchanged by a day of life? 31 May 1963 will never occur in my lifetime. In accordance with an ancient maritime tradition, I am now a member of The Order of the Golden Dragon. My service record will so note.

But more has changed than the day. The weather is freshening as well. The wind has slowly increased to 23 knots and the waves to 5 feet.

1020 Set Typhoon condition IV, reference CINCPACFLT. Made preparations for heavy weather.

So it begins. Typhoon season in the Western Pacific. We are on the petticoats of Typhoon Polly. Storms are all designated by naming them after females. While I am unsure who made that decision, I am too wise to comment on the logic or rationale involved. Most storms do not become typhoons, but a number do so and we will be harassed. By the time we return in November, we will have transited the alphabet one and a half times to Anna Pauline. A typhoon is simply a hurricane that occurs in the Pacific rather than the Atlantic. In the Pacific, the winds rotate in a clockwise direction in excess of 64 knots.

"Preparation for heavy weather." Topside, any loose gear is stowed in lockers. Loose gear might become deadly missiles. All hatches are dogged down securely. An open hatch may prove as catastrophic as a shell hole during battle. Similar action is taken within. In the Wardroom officers' mess, the signs of increasing foul weather are more subtle, but progressive. The first sign of weather is a damp tablecloth on the Wardroom table. As weather worsens, out come the fiddle boxes, wooden rectangular boxes designed to contain the dinnerware and fitted to each place. Ultimately, all pretense of meals halts. The steward's mates make sandwiches if possible and leave them in the refrigerator. Ultimately, we are lucky if we can retrieve a roll of bologna and a loaf of bread from which to tear off chunks between waves.

We begin to adjust our course to the southwest to avoid the worst of the storm. While this adjustment may save us from the worst of the weather, it will cost us three days ashore in Yokosuka, Japan.

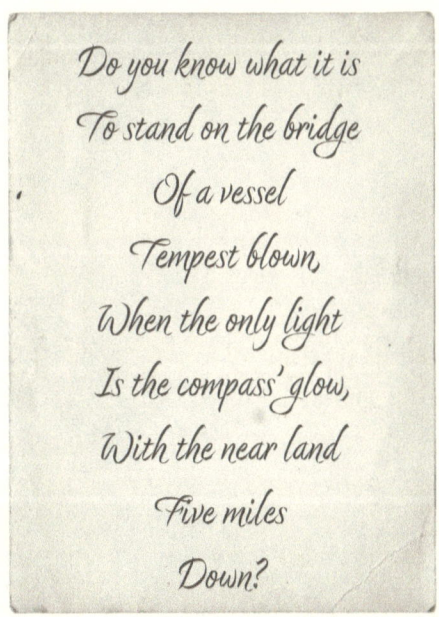

Do you know what it is
To stand on the bridge
Of a vessel
Tempest blown,
When the only light
Is the compass' glow,
With the near land
Five miles
Down?

YOKOSUKA I

Friday, 7 June 1963

As we skirt nature's disaster, Typhoon Polly, we continue to prepare for man's calamity, war. For the last week at sea, we have exercised at general quarters daily, never knowing when the alarm might sound, calling us to battle stations. We have fired live ammunition at target drones in the air, target sleds on the sea and spent a few rounds at nothing, just to show the Commodore we could. We even scrambled for genuine Anti-Submarine Warfare general quarters when sonar detected a suspicious contact. Ultimately the blip was identified as a whale, and a presumed noncombatant.

But now, Japan lies just below the horizon, betrayed only by a low haze. We are bound for Yokosuka on the Island of Honshu, home to Tokyo, Hiroshima, and Mount Fuji. Japan is a chain of volcanic islands strung together like a giant salamander. The northernmost island, Hokkaido, is the head, nearly touching its ancient enemy, Russia. The tail, Kyushu, trails south and east, resting upon the Sea of Japan, pretending to ignore, yet coveting the resources of the mainland.

As we approach, the land mass becomes visible, an apparition, slowly rising from the waters, as it did in the eons before man counted time. It is all soft greens and rugged browns below the cloud line. And then the scent, the essence of the land commingled with that of humanity, reaches the nostrils. It is the perfume of flora and fauna, of wood smoke and spice, of paddy fields and benjo ditches. It is the most sensual of odors and will excite me so long as I draw breath and remember.

As the land draws nearer, it forms itself into a rugged volcanic coastline. Unlike Hawaii, where the vegetation seems effortless as it enfolds the islands, Japan's trees seem to grasp and cling to the cliffs like scenes from an ancient wood cut.

0745 The shrill of a bosun's pipe over the 1MC precedes the order to set the special and anchor detail. We enter Sagami Wan, the larger bay leading into Tokyo Bay.

0955 We pass Fort Number 2 abeam to starboard. Along with Fort Number 4, it is one of the sentinels guarding the entrance to Tokyo Bay. Both of these were islands fully manned and armed to the teeth on 30 August 1945 when the first elements of the victorious combatants began to test carefully the veracity of Japanese surrender. When told of the surrender, it is reported that a dubious Bull Halsey ordered, "…cease firing, but if you see any enemy planes in the air shoot them down in a friendly manner."

As we enter Sagami Wan, I am standing on the foc'sle with Chief Sager and the rest of the 1st Division Bosun Mates. Sager is now my "Chief Marble." His 30 years supposedly taking orders from my 24 months. I can drive the ship and shoot the guns. I do reports and let him do the job.

As we steam toward Tokyo Bay, Sager tells of the first time he made this passage. "We was the first unit in after the Japs surrendered. We was to spike all the fixed artillery pointed at the entrance to Tokyo Bay. There was 19" guns along the ridges on both sides and they was bore sighted to spots in the bay, so's they could just blast anythin passin the spot. Them and those two damned forts were passin. Fish ina barrel, ducks ona pond. Take a look at that shoreline. Howd ya like to climb those cliffs with a pack an the Japs firin down at ya? Some fault Truman fur droppin those bombs, but I'd like ta see em try to take these home islands. Evn the civilians armed with axes and shovels…Hundreds of thousans dead on both sides. The used ta draw the Japs as little yella bastards, but them imperial Japs that took the Philippines was six feet tall." Sager does not eat sushi.

This is not CHEVY'S first visit to Tokyo Bay. Eighteen years ago, she was a part of the victory fleet anchored about the "Mighty Mo," USS MISSOURI, upon whose gray decks the chastened Japanese dignitaries stood, awaiting the pleasure of the new emperor, General Douglas MacArthur. Her decks were mottled with clusters of white and khaki uniforms. The officers dressed in traditional open necked working khaki, mingled with seamen in liberty whites, all straining toward the capitulation. MacArthur had ordered that the officers be dressed in the same attire in which they had fought. The ceremony took place one level above the main deck and just aft of one of the massive forward 16" gun batteries whose long barrels were elevated at the 45 degree ready. Sailors, officers, and representatives of the Allied forces crowded every inch, clinging to life lines and perched on gun mounts, all focused on a small table at which the Japanese ambassador, clad in black tails, sat signing away his country's sovereignty, beneath the gaze of a towering MacArthur. "Where the hell are the planes?" demanded Bull Halsey. At that moment, the sky turned black. Low flew the 450 planes from the carrier fleet followed by the B-29s in formation. Overseeing the proceedings from afar, stood Fujisan, Mt. Fuji, sacred mountain, chastened but eternal.

But today is overcast with no sign of Fujisan as we begin our approach to the Yokosuka Naval Shipyard. All engines are stopped as 6 US Navy LCMs come alongside to act as pusher boats in our landing process. No self-respecting destroyer captain would allow this crutch. We are the "cowboys," the "greyhounds of the sea." We are seamen, we land our own vessels. But we are in a foreign port, and it is the harbor pilot's choice, as he navigates the prickle of cranes and masts that are his shipyard.

1143 We are moored to Pier 6 in a nest of four destroyers. It is Friday, 7 June 1963. We have been at sea for the best part of three weeks. I have had one warm beer on Midway since leaving Hawaii. I am ready to step onto my first foreign shore.

The first step, however, is reflex for a sailor. A US Naval installation looks much the same in Japan as it does in the United States. It is a clutter of piers alongside of which reside warships in various stages of replenishment and repair. Yokosuka's main distinguishing feature was the second largest crane in the world towering above the various units of the US 7th Fleet, declaring this facility once a place of building ships for the emperor.

The first stop will always be the Officers' Club for alcohol, a meal, and anticipation. Here we are allowed to exchange our MPC's, Military Payment Certificate, Mickey Mouse Money, sailors' pay, for yen. "Yen," an ironic unit of exchange for men who have been at sea for three weeks.

Yokosuka, as a city, is remarkable only in that it is a puzzle to solve. In ports around the world, the neighborhood by a base caters to sailors and laborers. There is no great beauty. While it is cluttered and crammed, it is not squalid. For a city separated from devastation by eighteen years, there are no piles of rubble, no sign of conflict. The men of great titles and ambition surrendered. The people who bear the burden of the great shrugged and rebuilt their lives. There is no apparent animosity. We are treated as friends, or more realistically, as commercial opportunities. Yokosuka is, however, a corridor through which to pass to the beauty of the countryside. It is a wellspring and receptacle of human experience.

Since departing CONUS (Continental United States), the WESTPAC (Western Pacific) vets have begun to sprinkle daily conversation with Japanese, or derivatives thereof. I am now "budsan," honorific of Mister Bud. "Arigato," thanks. "Dozo," please. Just a little more is a "Skosh," derivative of "Sukoshi. "Dai jobu," O.K. "Ah so," That's right. "Ichi ban," Number one." "Takusan," Much, large amount. "Josan," girl, girlfriend. "Your josan is dai jobee, she has takusan"...you get the idea.

We, the uninitiated, have been tantalized with tales of certain wonders of the Orient as well as by the jargon. One of the most fabled experiences is the "Hotsie Bath," literally, hot bath or hot massage. Yokosuka is home to my first "Hotsie" experience. Put aside carnal thoughts. This traditional Japanese bath is much more about the water than the women.

To truly understand the allure of the Hotsie, one must first understand the "Destroyer Shower." The means of CHEVY'S propulsion is steam, the source of which is water. Underway, CHEVY distills her own pure propulsion from the sea. All other uses—cooking, drinking, laundry and bathing—are secondary. Daily consumption is closely monitored. Showers represent the epitome of constraint. The shower in Forward Officers is coffin-sized. I place myself squarely before the head grasping each water control. I rotate both levers simultaneously. There is no adjustment. The objective is to dampen my body before the water reaches the deck. The water is turned off while I attempt to lather my most critical parts. The rinse is a replication of process one. In a perfectly executed shower, the deck is not damp. The body was tantalized, but scummy. Repeat the destroyer douche daily for one to two weeks in the WESTPAC summer, and you will understand the allure of infinite quantities of hot water. Then add a lithe Japanese maiden clad in white shorts and blouse, and you begin to understand the attraction of the Baths after two weeks at sea.

The uniform of the day is a white towel about the waist. The process commences in a steam cabinet, during which one's brow is constantly assuaged by a damp cloth in the hand of one's maiden of the day. One is then showered, scrubbed, and finally dunked to soak, neck deep in a tub of hot water. Any scrubbing of private parts is accompanied by a damp sponge and a "dozo," please wash your own parts. The finale is a full body massage, professionally performed by one's masseuse. The size of the women is such that to loosen the deep muscles of one's back and buttocks, they must walk on your back utilizing a heel to toe rhythm. Ah, for the patter of little feet on one's spine.

Back to sea.

TICONDEROGA

Thursday 13 June 1963

Steaming in company with Task Group 77.5 composed of USS TICONDEROGA (CVA 14) USS MCKEAN (DDR 784), USS CHEVALIER (DD 805) AND USS TOWERS (DDG 9). Operating off the southern coast of Japan. Formation course is 200 degrees. Steaming a darkened ship with the exception of running lights.

Signed,

E.P. Mackey, LTJG, USNR

I have the Midwatch. The Messenger of the Watch woke me thirty minutes ago, reported that the temperature was about 80 degrees and cloudy, ascertained that I was awake, and then departed to rouse the remainder of the watch section. I pulled on working khakis, climbed the ladder one deck up to the Wardroom, checked to see if the stewards had left any of their "giligili" in the fridge, and settled for a bologna sandwich and milk. At this time, the Wardroom is bathed in a red light. The purpose, to nurture night vision. The effect, to render the familiar setting surreal. I climb one level to the bridge and review the night orders and ship's status with the OOD, Doug Biddle. I glance over the formation. We three destroyers are headed mostly south running interference for the TICONDEROGA, astern about three miles. When I am convinced that I understand the situation and orders, I salute Doug and declare, "I relieve you, sir." He responds, "I stand relieved." As he heads for his rack, I inform the watch, "Mr. Mackey, I have the Conn." With that assertion, I assume responsibility to the Captain and the US Navy for the performance of CHEVALIER and the safety of her officers and crew.

Three decks below the bridge, the bowels of CHEVY contain her four steam-producing boilers and the engine room watch. Steam drives the turbines, turning the massive twin brass propellers that thrust us through the sea. If the "screws" are the muscle, then the bridge is the brain of CHEVALIER. The bridge contains the eyes and ears of the ship, both human and electronic. But it is the human brain that must process that which the electronics provide. The bridge is the final receptor of radio communication, radar impulse, and sonar echoes. Data from these sources passes to the watch in CIC (Combat Information Center) and the bridge. If the carrier orders a course change, coming into the wind to launch or recover aircraft, CIC will calculate the adjustment and recommend a course and speed to the OOD. But it is the OOD who must decide to give the order to the helmsman to change course and send the ordered speed to the engine room watch. While it takes a team to drive a ship, only the OOD has the power and responsibility to give the order to execute. There is no democracy, only expediency. There is no vote.

In a 24-hour day, I will be one of four OODs. We will each spend an average of six hours on the bridge. When the carrier is in flight launch or recovery mode, the watch is action and stress. If the watch falls between midnight and dawn, there is time to observe and reflect, so long as the ocean allows. When she is mellow, we reflect. When she is in a temper, she besieges us with waves taller than the masts, winds that tear at the rigging and blow the tops from the waves in a stinging pique. Then we just hang on and keep our bow into the sea.

Her mood tonight is tolerable, but there is a caution in the winds that have increased out of the south to twenty knots. The sea remains comfortable, but the tempestuous Shirley lurks somewhere to the south, with course and landfall to be determined by her caprice.

Our task at the moment is to wear out the night and await TICONDEROGA'S pleasure in the dawn. We three screening destroyers are sweeping clean her course into the night. We are so positioned that the conical search of our sonars intersect invisibly beneath the surface to test her way for hostile submarines. Chinese or Russian, both inhabit these waters. We are in the East China Sea off the Ryukyu Islands and headed for the Formosa Straits, so the best bet would be Chinese. But both adversaries are hostile and Communist in the current Cold War. The Soviets patrol these waters as well and have better subs.

Ahead we steam, scanning the depths for danger. We would take torpedoes, as our duty, in the service of our carrier and country.

From the wing of the bridge, I can trace the rhythmic rock of my sister destroyers' running lights in the distance. All is quiet, as the sea swallows most sounds but her own. The hull resonates with the vibrations of our engines. The circular radar scope in the pilot house illuminates the outline of Ryukyu as the cursor caresses her shore, and then flashes in a brief fluorescent burst, as her reflected waves touch the bulk of TICONDEROGA. Sleep well, world.

TICONDEROGA
UNDERWAY

14 June – 21 June 1963

14 June 1963

The Ryukyus are better recognized for the historic Okinawa, site of the final amphibious landing of WWII and possibly its most brutal. The attack began on April Fool's day in 1945 and lasted an inhuman 82 days. From this vantage, daily air strikes were launched over the Emperor's home islands.

But we are here for more current issues. The Ryukyus are adjacent to the Taiwan Straits, troubled waters since Mao forced Chang and the routed Nationalists from the mainland to the island of Taiwan. On a chart, Taiwan resembles a giant dog turd plopped off the coast. Mao would probably concur. We have formally and informally patrolled the straits since the 1950s in support of Non-Communist China. The historic flashpoints in the straits are a pair of small islands located between the two militants, Matsu and Quemoy, known also as Kinmun. In the early 50s, the Nationalists on the island and the Communists on the mainland began shelling one another daily. In 1958, through some inscrutable form of Oriental logic, the sides determined that they would take turns shelling one another on alternate days and that the shells would deliver propaganda leaflets rather than high explosives. The alternate day shelling continues to this day, as does our presence in the straits. Ironically, it was early in the dispute that it was discovered that our fleet was armed only with nukes and without conventional capability. It was nukes or nothing. We now patrol with conventional weapons.

So our current assignment is to fly the flag. We continue to splash about the East China Sea, screening the TICONDEROGA and doing our gas and grocery shopping from the oilers (AOs) and reefers (ARs) assigned to replenish our Task Group at sea.

19 June 1200-1600

We seem typhoon-free for a while. The sun is shining, the temperature is in the low 80s, and the sea is as flat as it gets with two-foot waves. In carrier pilot speak, it is "CAVU," CEILING AND VISIBILITY UNLIMITED. The Task Group has settled into a rhythm of preparedness and practice. We have spent the last week carving our wakes from East China to the Philippine Sea and back. Launching aircraft which go, we know not where, to return, be recovered, refueled, and prepared to do it all again tomorrow. We are an undisguised threat whose fist is the TICONDEROGA. She is the hive and her aircraft the sting.

For the moment we bide our time and maintain station. The afternoon launch is complete and will not return until the 2000 to 2400 watch. I stand on the wing of the bridge watching two A4 Skyhawk fighters make live rocket runs on a target towed to the east of the TYCO.

How to explain an aircraft carrier? She is roughly the size of 20 CHEVALIERS. Her flight deck towers four stories above the sea's surface. Her island and bridge rise an additional three stories above the flight deck. Three football fields would rest comfortably on her deck. She is home to 3500 souls and 100 aircraft of various sizes and missions. Imagine Soldier Field or a city block traveling at 40 MPH on the surface of the Pacific. But sheer bulk belies her military might. She is called TICONDEROGA after the revolution's triumphant battle. Even armed with conventional weapons, she is a battle, or a small war unto herself. One of her fighter bombers alone carries the punch of a WWII battleship. Then think of non-conventional nuclear. But all this power might yet be neutralized by several strategically placed torpedoes. That is why we encircle the TYCO with our necklace of steel and sound.

While Captain Stanko respects the carriers, he sees in them a limitation with respect to certain indigenous peoples. A small African nation purchased the home behind his as their embassy in D.C. and commenced having ethnic celebrations late into some evenings. Since then, his tolerance for the nations of that continent has become somewhat jaded. "We should never have mothballed the battleships. That bunch of spear rattling natives can't understand the subtlety of a carrier. They need to see a ship bristling with 16-inch guns to get the picture."

The order comes from TYCO to change course. At the order to "execute," we "cowboys" scramble for our newly assigned stations. My radar scope is illuminated with our electronic reflections like those of a half dozen startled fireflies on a field of fluorescent green.

Friday, 21 June 0000-0400

In the past ten days, we have steamed over 2600 peripatetic miles in the nation's service. I have been drenched by towering waves at the typhoon's pleasure, coated in fuel oil the consistency of mud, compliments of a broken fueling connection. Appropriately baptized into the brotherhood of cold warriors.

The sea is friendly, the breeze fresh, and the moon's imprint is a golden goblet on the ocean's canvas.

Today we moor in Osaka.

OSAKA

Monday, 24 June 1963, 1800-2400

2102 Secured from night plane guard station and lighting measure green. 1500 yards directly astern, tailing TYCO like a dog and master, she fills much of my horizon. I watch as the last of her returning fighters sink like somnolent fireflies to their flight deck. The A-3 Skywarrior roars low above, guided by my masthead light to the waiting flight deck ahead. The bomber, the size of a medium commercial airliner, is always the last to land and signals the close of night ops.

E arly this morning, we let slip our lines and carefully felt our way through the mists of Osaka Wan, our foghorn moaning its measured complaint to any craft willing to listen. As the port awakens with the dawn, the bay is still and the air is pungent with spice, wood smoke, and humanity. Visibility is limited, and ghost craft flit in and out of our vision like weekend memories. A host of bum boats skitter about us like Jesus Bugs to bid us farewell. One of the boats, I am informed, contains a group of ladies who seem to have found temporary true love with members of the crew.

Osaka nestles on the chart next to Yokohama, south of Tokyo. It is one of the largest cities in the world of which you have not heard. Like our Detroit, it is a maker of autos and collateral commodities. Surely blue collar, though in its case there are no blue collars. As such, it lacks the tourist appeal of Tokyo to the north or Kobe, slightly west.

As a ship of lesser seniority, we drew the short straw, and we were sent to Osaka. The Commodore assigned TYCO and TOWERS to the more desirable port of Kobe across the bay. This entire area was heavily bombed during WWII, and the people of Japan are the only population ever subject to atomic devastation. The citizens take nuclear weaponry quite seriously. TYCO and TOWERS, with their nuclear might (though armed with only conventional weaponry), were picketed by anti-nuclear activists. Their officers and crew spent the weekend confined to quarters. Take that, Commodore.

Osaka is a port and as such, its waterfront is populated with the alcohol and willing women all ports have in common. But a little beyond the ships and neon lies a real Japan, surviving and enduring.

While Yokosuka's primary imprint is that of the United States Navy, Osaka is a port of the world. Most of the people of Osaka have never seen an American Naval Officer or a US Naval vessel. We were a curiosity, not an enemy. What little Japanese I thought I had seemed a foreign language in Osaka. If one ventured out of sight of the port, one was well advised to do so with a match pack from one of the prominent local bars with address imprinted. Shown to one of the city cab drivers, that and a few hundred yen might see you home and not AWOL.

Riding behind the driver of a Japanese tour bus is reminiscent of the front seat on a roller coaster. The difference being, there might well be another car on the same track headed our way. We are headed for Takarazuka. The area is located just outside Tokyo and combines a zoo, mini Disneyland, and a world-famous, all-female theater dance troupe. The young women are literally indentured to the company for their careers. The dancers troop from their quarters, across a small bridge to the theater. This bridge was made famous by James Michener in his novel *Sayonara*. It was known by the GIs as the "Bitchie Bashi," literally the "Bitches' Bridge," or bridge of the women.

We are oddities wherever we go, partly because we are required to wear our tropical white uniforms. Someone in the upper echelons decided that we would be safer in our uniforms than not. At 6'2" and 210 lbs., I stand head and shoulders above the average Japanese street crowd and am not difficult to spot as a non-Asian "round eye." The white uniform simply makes me a better target. But that is not an issue. While our brother officers are picketed in Kobe, we are beloved photo opportunities.

It is Saturday, and throngs of visitors crowd the parks. Many are clusters of young students, the boys in white shirts and blue shorts, the girls in blue pleated skirts and white sailor fuku tops. All are led by a vigilant teacher, protectress, and mentor. Cameras are everywhere. Sometimes it seems the nation is staring at the world through large lens Nikons. My personal camera is palm sized with no discernible lens and acquired from the ship's store afloat in Yokosuka. It draws curious and perhaps sympathetic stares. My favorite picture is of a diminutive schoolteacher having her picture taken between two towering naval officers in white, as her students stare in awe.

Sunday, another tour bus. This time to Kyoto, an ancient city of shrines and the Golden Pagoda, built as a residence in the late thirteenth century. Now a Zen Temple, it is truly golden, resting on stilts at the edge of a wooded pond.

Kyoto, adjacent to Tokyo, was initially considered by planners a prime target for our atomic bomb. As a religious and cultural center, it was felt the citizenry could better appreciate and convey to the nation the awful nature of the weapon. It was spared. Hiroshima was sacrificed instead.

But in the low hills of the city rests a newer temple. Like the USS ARIZONA, it is a place for remembrance, a prayer for peace. It is a simple one-storied structure, but atop the temple sits the Ryozen Kannon, Buddhist goddess of peace. The eighty-foot concrete goddess is framed by the low green hills behind, beneath a canopy of pure blue sky. She sits gazing into the reflecting pond before her and eternity beyond. As she sits, she meditates upon tablets beneath her commemorating the death of two million Japanese soldiers and a single tablet to the Unknown Soldier.

I was granted two days to discover something of the real Japan. But I will remember them well. I will remember uniformed school children trooping through ancient parks. People of all ages playing baseball. A young boy politely asking if he might practice his English. A young girl's smile. A laugh of approval, as a man ventures "Thank you," and the officer offers, "Domo aregato." A kimonoed hostess, kneeling at our table, playing "You are My Sunshine" on her samisen. A young boy in a Yankees cap grinning, "I like Americans." As we slip through the mists of Osaka Wan escorted by bum boats, I will remember. And I will remember the goddess.

GODDESS

Reclining

In a bamboo and paper room,

Suffused with sandalwood and sweat,

The broad brown face

With almond eyes,

Watching, watching.

Pockmarked goddess

Of the Orient

Resigned, resilient.

Enduring,

Eternal Earth Mother.

YOKOSUKA II

Wednesday, 26 June 1963, 1600-1800

Still sailing at the whim of TICONDEROGA and CINCPACFLT in the sea of Japan, our martial ballet becoming ever more synchronized. On the surface, our forces reorient smartly about TYCO as we prowl the Pacific. We are an iron fist, not a pointed finger. Aboard CHEVALIER, the acts of replenishing and combat are efficient routine rather than studied response. This afternoon we were detached for anti-aircraft exercise. My gunners fired eighty effective rounds of AA bursts in record time. We have returned to the formation and have settled into the rescue station 1500 yards astern of the carrier. While not in contentious waters, we remain vigilant. We will not journey far, as we are scheduled to weekend in Yokosuka.

Yesterday was mail day. At sea our mailman flies a small Bell helicopter. Matching our course and speed, he hovers above our fantail, and then lowers the mail bag to my waiting bosun mates. The pilot was a classmate from Princeton. There was a letter for me from home. Both surprises.

With time before my next watch, I went below to Forward Officers with my prize. On board ship, there is no news of the world, especially news of home. Some news is more welcome than others, however. Pat is missing.

I am something of a loner. I keep my own counsel. I plot my own course. I guess that is why I live in Forward Officers with Dick Hart. I like people, but I know better than to get too close. Since birth, my average residence in any place has been about two and a half years. My four years at Princeton, my longest established address. I do not share my emotions with anyone. I seek refuge in the pages of books; pen and paper are my solace.

I have had one constant friend since the age of ten, but he has vanished. Pat is missing without a trace. No one has seen him, nor has his body been found. Pat was unwanted, too big, too black to be acceptable. So he came to me as a four-month Kerry Blue Terrier pup, the exiled prince of a show dog litter. He was a dude, a rascal, with a terrier attitude and all of his male parts. When I ran the fields or prowled the woods, he was beside me. When I acquired my prized red Schwinn Cruiser, he was my outrider. When I lost my bone-handled jackknife, he helped me look. When Sally gave my I.D. bracelet back, he let me hug him and watched as I flung it into the woods, vowing to never love again. When I got my driver's license, he would ride shotgun in the front seat of my '53 Ford convertible. He had just been groomed, always his finest hour. Even at fourteen, he would strut like the pick of the litter he was. And he vanished. Perhaps he simply ascended to that place reserved for all true canine spirits. I wish him green fields and good hunting. I hope his ascent was swift and painless. Sit. Stay. Rest.

Saturday, 29 June 1963

Jim Porter, you burr-cut, red-headed, ass-kissing, brown-nosing SOB. You have the temerity to think BROWN is actually an Ivy League school. "What's the color of horse shit? Brown, Brown, Brown." Temporary Department Head. You even managed to graduate below me from OCS, which was not easy. I outrank you.

Some days should not happen. I am not Christian, I am not forgiving. I will not love my enemy. If I turn my cheek it will be only to spit more directly into his eye. Jim Porter, my acting department head. Avoid me, Jim. You are a good officer and I trust you on the bridge. We could be friends, but we are two alphas. Don't cross me. You are temporary.

Don Cunningham, you are a mustang Lieutenant with twenty years in. They are transferring you to the hospital after one month's sea duty for being chronically seasick? You are my friend, my mentor in the ways of Japan. Say it is not so, but you cannot, for you are gone. Sayonara, Donsan. Gomenasai, sorry. And I am left with Porter.

We are back in Yokosuka, moored with our sister destroyers, alongside the tender PIEDMONT (AD 17).

But the ways of the Bureau of Personnel are mysterious. They have turned over the majority of our Wardroom since leaving San Diego. They have taken the XO, the OPS Officer, and the Gun Boss off the top. Ensigns Gardner Randell and John Enrud of the USNR reported aboard today. Our new XO arrived as we tied up in Yokosuka as well. LTCDR Campbell, straight from the academy in Annapolis. While the enlisted ranks and CPOs are stable, the Wardroom sometimes seems a turnstile. Who knows what the Ouijas in BUPERS will send us for a new Weapons Officer?

But my life is newly complicated. As I now head the 1st and 2nd Divisions, I have gained two green Ensigns. Ensign Risley with my Gunners Mates and FTs is goofy and I suspect Packard with the Bosun Mates is not too bright. Thank God for my CPOs. Good luck, Chiefs. I have also been informed that when we arrive in Subic, we will board six college senior Midshipmen for the month. These, I will inherit as the newly anointed "Midshipmen Liaison Officer." Just call me "Father Goose." Oh, and I have also been designated "Counterinsurgency Officer" and handed ten pounds of study manuals compliments of the Naval War College of Correspondence. My, what will I do with all my spare time? Join the Navy, stay on board.

More news. The idiosyncratic Naval Supply System has struck again. Waiting on the quay was a 200-pound motor for a gunnery practice loading machine. I requisitioned this replacement item during our refitting in Long Beach in early 1962. The motors are either "right-handed" or "left-handed." For the third time we have been sent a left-handed motor for our right-handed machine. I am convinced that some day after I return to civilian life, a 200-pound left-handed motor will arrive on my doorstep. Doug Biddle asserts that the entire system is run by "little old ladies in tennis shoes." He swears that once a frustrated recreation officer was forced to submit a requisition for equipment entitled "Balls, pong, ping."

Tonight I will seek sustenance at the Officers' Club in the form of a Kobe steak and drown my frustration in Asahi beer. Ironic, as Kobe steers are fattened on Asahi beer and hand massaged for tenderness. The sailors have a wry take on Asahi, which is consumed from liter-sized bottles at the local bars in Thieves Alley. They have christened Japan the land of "knee-high women and ass-high beer."

At night, Thieves Alley bursts on the senses as neon fireworks. The Black Rose, the Club Yokosuka, purveyors of the booze and breasts that draw the fleet, are no place for commissioned officers. After supper, I will run a few quarters through the slot machines, and then buy a fifth of Jim Beam from the O Club liquor store. The Clover Club, the CHEVY officers' refuge in Yokosuka, is a short Datsun cab ride from the naval base. The club is located on the second floor of a nondescript building in a quiet neighborhood. It is a haven equipped with a classic jukebox and dance floor. The music is largely American pop, with Japanese favorites and some European offerings thrown in. Goro is the proprietor. "Goro-san, iceu, mizu, kudasai." Goro will show us to a table, provide ice and water for our whiskey, and then add a hostess for each man if there is no "special friend." If Goro's choice is not acceptable, another josan is immediately presented. At military curfew, the party simply moves to "Hibachi side," a private club on the same floor.

But tonight there will be no Hibachi side for me. Tomorrow I intend to strike out on my own to discover Japan. I will head for the train station (eki) and attempt to purchase a round trip ticket to Kamakura. With some luck, I will not end up AWOL somewhere in northern Honshu.

KAMAKURA

Sunday, 30 June 1963

There and back. Round trip. I cannot say it in Japanese, but my pocket Japanese book and I made the journey.

The countryside flits by the train window like the film-strip of a travelogue. Forty minutes on the train and four centuries in time. I arrive in a vintage village without "gaijin," foreigners. No military, no residue of occupation. I am probably the only American in the area, and certainly on the train.

Kamakura is a seaside village on Sagami Wan, to which the Japanese retreat from the density of Tokyo. Its most ancient and revered inhabitant is "The Great Buddha." Unlike the "Goddess of Peace," this Buddha is ancient bronze dating to the fifteenth century. His scarred visage is one of stern sadness, perhaps in contemplation of the intransigence of man to the lessons of the past four hundred years.

Waiting at the station is a most unlikely representative of the local Chamber of Commerce. He is shod in calf-high black rubber boots. Clad in khaki shorts and a tee shirt, he stands a bit over five feet. Mounted on this diminutive frame is a Cheshire smile and a black eye patch. A motorcycle with a sidecar is by his side. He is waving at me as if waiting for my arrival.

He has little English, and I less Japanese, but we strike a deal. Deals are easy, even on Navy pay, where 10,000 yen is about $27. We are instant friends. With me seated in the sidecar of his motorized rickshaw, we are off to tour the shrines and temples of Kamakura. The system is simple. We visit a point of interest. He positions me for an appropriate photo, and then onward. After a few stops, he would shout "sake-ba" over the roar of his motorcycle. That indicated that it was time to refresh. A "sake-ba" is literally translated as a neighborhood tavern. We would stop, share a liter of Asahi beer to cut the road dust, and be on our way. At one point, he called out "soba-ya," a noodle shop, and we had lunch.

By late afternoon, we had visited enough shrines, drunk enough beer, and bought enough prayers to save our souls for at least a day. Back at the station, we shake hands, hug, and speak "sayonara." We must have seemed unlikely friends to the boarding passengers. As the train slid into the dusk toward Yokosuka, I could see him waving from the station platform. I have a roll of film and his "business card." He is older than I, I think. I am sure he was more touched by the war than I. I wonder how much? But we are friends. On this glorious Sunday in June, we were caught in the act of being. Of being alive and celebrating the only June 30, 1963 that will ever be.

INDEPENDENT STEAMING

2 July 1963, underway for Subic Bay, Philippine Islands

O700 We steer various courses and speeds, standing out of Tokyo Bay. The temperature is in the high 70s and low clouds still obscure Fujisan, omniscient in the mists. The sensuous odor of the land yields to the smell of the freshening sea.

Once clear of the harbor, we set a westerly course. I think the Captain is ready to be on his own for a while, as we kick it up to twenty knots, leaving the Land of the Rising Sun in our rapidly spreading wake.

It may be that the Captain has personal issues on his mind. He is in the zone for promotion. The next stripe would make him a full Captain, Captain in rank as well as title. The U.S. honors each man who commands a vessel, large or small, with the title "Captain." But the fourth stripe must be won through service, performance, and perhaps some politics. He must contend with the other officers in his zone for promotion to a limited number of jobs. Promotion is a pyramid, with only one Chief of Naval Operations at the top. "Passed Over" once, try again. "Passed

Over" twice, you are retired. Captain Stanko has been passed over once.

For the present, Captain Stanko and the USS *Chevalier* are heading south. No carriers, no screens, or flight ops. Just blessed independent steaming to our next assignment. Our next stop will be the U.S. Naval base in Subic Bay. Over the next five days, we will transit roughly the distance from San Francisco to Acapulco, with corresponding changes in temperature. We are headed for the "Dog Days" in the "Horse Latitudes." It is going to get sticky in Forward Officers.

Wednesday, 3 July 1963

LCDR Campbell, armed with his sextant, is pleased, as the last two nights have provided excellent visibility for shooting the stars. We know where we are in the Pacific, which is a good thing in a large body of water.

LCDR Campbell joined us in Yokosuka, replacing LCDR Gabriel as XO. As with most XOs, it is easier to know when he is displeased than pleased. We have yet to get a fix on him. ENS Simmons was at the Naval Academy while Campbell was assigned to the staff there. It is not encouraging to learn that the Midshipmen nicknamed him "Soupy," but then, Simmons may have had a nickname as well. Time will tell, but for the rest of the cruise, "Soupy" or not, he will be our shipmate, XO, and navigator.

0000–0400 Steaming independently into the new day, in accordance with the COMSEVENTHFLT OP Schedule. Captain Stanko is commander of everything. He is in his sea cabin, aft of the bridge. The ship is darkened, except for running lights. The crew is at rest, but for the bridge watch, the engine room and cooks in the gallery.

You cannot know the ocean from its edges,
Looking out to sea from the stability shore.
From shore, it is the ocean that moves,
While man stands firmly on the strand.
On a small ship, it is man who moves,
To the undulant rhythm of the deep.
No watcher he, but supplicant.
Subject to her whims and rages,
Surrounded by horizon,
as he slips beneath the edge of the world.
When he dared look into its heart,
He glimpsed a time most ancient.
He shivered as the breath of God
Awoke the Deep with a sigh.
Before the heavens,
Before the land,
Before Man's time,
There was the sea.

We continue westerly at twenty knots through a flat sea. When I catch my next watch, 1600–1800, the Deck Log will still read, "Steaming as before." I stand alone on the starboard wing of the bridge, my shipmates secure and gentle breeze on my face. No better time to reflect.

"They know the works of the Lord and see His wonders in the deep..."

Standing on the bridge in mid-ocean, I can literally see the world curve downward at the horizon around me. When a ship appears, the first thing I see is the tip of its masts. The hull then slowly rises to sight as if emerging from the depths. From above, my ship is but a flick of dust on a pristine surface. This night, I am surrounded by a hemisphere of stars and planets. God's planetarium.

A LETTER HOME

Dear Family,

Happy 4th of July. I guess for you, it is still 3 July, but it will be at least a week before you are likely to get this letter. Since we are not operating with a carrier group, the nearest mailbox will be in Subic Bay, a few days hence.

We are currently in the Philippine Sea, just south of Okinawa. If there are spots on this page, they are sweat, not tears. There is no A/C in Forward Officers' Country and the blowers merely move the humidity around. Men of iron and ships of steel sweat in the tropics.

This afternoon, the Captain declared "Holiday Routine" for all hands not in the duty section. At 1400 hours (2:00 PM), all hands assembled on the "Flight Deck" for a "Smoker." A few cigarettes were evident, but the liquid refreshment was limited to black coffee. With the exception of a medical supply, no alcohol is permitted on a US Naval warship. It was a unique gathering, as normally enlisted men and commissioned officers do not fraternize. Even on a small ship, Officer's Country, Chief Petty Officer's Quarters and Enlisted Men's spaces are havens to each. But the Navy has its ceremonies and customs.

"Flight Deck" is something of a misnomer, as we have nothing aboard that flies but the occasional seagull. We are supposed to have a pair of DASH remote controlled helicopters, but they have yet to be released to the fleet by BUWEPS. Even if we had them, we have no one qualified to maintain or fly them and no weapons with which to arm them. The proposed arms, however, are interesting. The "bird" is capable of carrying either homing torpedoes or depth charges. The idea is that the drone will be vectored above a sonar contact and release its weapon, rather than having the ship move to the presumed submarine as in the WWII movies. The choice of weapon is also interesting; as our arsenal could presumably include a nuclear depth charge. If that is the selection, we might accidentally nuke Moby Dick or start WWIII.

What we do have is the flight deck and hangar, compliments of our FRAM conversion. The hangar and flight deck are just aft of the stacks one level above the main deck, where an aft gun mount was formerly located. The hangar is roughly the size of a large two-car garage with a high ceiling. The flight deck measures about 30' x 40'. With the roller door raised, and a movie screen suspended at the opening, a film can be shown with the crew seated outside in fair weather and inside the hangar in foul weather. The same arrangement is available for Sunday services, which are not as well attended as the movies.

Today the screen is down, not to show a film, but to obscure the waiting entertainers from the waiting audience. Along the port side of the deck, chairs have been arranged for the CO, XO, and Senior Chief Petty Officer. The remainder of the crew and officers arrange themselves along the lifelines surrounding the hangar deck. Nearly everyone present was both viewer and participant.

Barnes, GMG1, was Master of Ceremonies. Attired in a red head bandana and one strap overalls, a creative uniform of the day, but strictly non-regulation. He looked like a hillbilly pirate.

DEDICATION

My memories are not of heroes of yore,

Who perished with grim resolution,

But rather of sailors who lived, joked and swore,

Through the sea's everyday evolution.

My heroes just jostled with everyday chores,

Without patriotic commotion.

Preparing for conflict or undeclared war,

On the sailing man's seven day ocean.

Those shadows who sweltered on Far Eastern seas,

And tossed with the typhoon unfurled,

The peacekeeping navy, who fought a cold war,

On the nakedest edge of the world.

For them I ask reflection,

And release

A prayer,

For those dared

The dangerous game

Of peace.

His opening was backed by a gunners mate and a torpedoman on electric guitars with a fire-control technician on the bongos.

As the afternoon progressed, an assortment of men and instruments made their way to the fore. Officers and men vied for supremacy in the "Twist," with ENS Rod Horn, US Naval Academy and TLJG Tom Womack, University of Texas, clad in Aloha shirts, representing the Wardroom. They did make a charming couple, but did not prevail.

The beauty contest for Miss South East Philippine Sea was a highlight. It is amazing what grown men without women will do to amuse themselves in the Pacific. None of the eight contestants weighed less than 180 lbs. Imagine Lovelace, GMG3, a 6' 275 lb. African maiden, turned out in a tasteful, black bikini, complete with breasts. ENS Russell, at 6'5", clad in a fetching flowered kimono and wearing eye shadow, towering over Barnes, looking more like a pagoda than a geisha.

The smoker ended with a chocolate cream pie eating contest… no hands, and the emptied tin must be turned upside down on the contestant's head. As a final indignity, the contestant must signal his completion with a shrill whistle. Ever attempted to whistle with a mouth full of pie crust?

No fireworks, no watermelon, but a Fourth of July I will remember for my lifetime. As the afternoon fades, the gods of war and peace look down and chuckle at the warriors' holiday.

SUBIC BAY I

Saturday 6 July 1963, Philippine Islands, 1200-1600 steaming as before

We have just sighted the Capones Island Light about ten miles off the port bow. The light has guided mariners to Subic Bay and Manila since 1890. Our Independence Day and blessed independent steaming are over.

The clouds are broken with occasional rain showers. The sea is a warm bath, at nearly ninety degrees. We approach the land and are cloaked in humidity and jungle smells, as if entering a tropical greenhouse. Grand Island and Ft. Wint slide down our port side. We enter the bay and the island spreads before us. Its volcanic mountains are cloud shrouded, with glimpses of brown and green rising and falling, to disappear in the blanketing cumulus. A long pier, backed by the low gray buildings and cranes of the ship repair facility, is visible ahead.

We moor in the bay, starboard side to the USS HECTOR (AR7) at Buoy 19. The port seems busy. Dockside space, some five hundred yards away, is crowded and limited to the more senior vessels. LCVPs will act as liberty craft rather than the landing boats they were two decades ago. We are an early arrival. Soon the bay will be full of the fleet, arriving to embark their quota of collegiate Midshipmen for the month.

"Welcome to the Alluvial Dung Heap," as Captain Stanko lovingly anoints The Philippines. "If the world had hemorrhoids, this is where it would bleed." He provides no specifics. I assume we will be left to draw our own conclusions. The Captain served on the submarine USS TARPON (SS175) during the latter stages of WWII in the Pacific. The brutality of the war in the Pacific was unspeakable, and I surmise the memories trouble him. But he laughs as he says it again, "Alluvial Dung Heap."

The Philippines is, in fact, a cluster of islands. These islands have been exploited by the Spanish, the Americans, and the Japanese, each in their own special way. Useless bravery, mindless brutality. The islands harbor tribes still living as in the Stone Age, while the prehistoric jungle obscures what little civilization encroaches. Welcome to Subic Bay and the metropolis of Olongapo.

After a light supper in the Wardroom, those officers not on duty forsake the CHEVY in search of distilled spirits and attitude adjustment. Independent steaming is a holiday from fleet ops. But it is grog free. We move in a khaki mass, clad in short-sleeved tropical uniform shirts and dress slacks. Olongapo is considered sufficiently dangerous that the Admiral has decreed that all military personnel, both officers and enlisted, be clad in the "uniform of the day" when ashore. Presumably, this means that if we are mugged or shot, the assault will be intentional rather than accidental. In a town of small brown people, one would think that being a large white "round eye" would be sufficient differentiation.

The captain has ordered his "gig" to transport us to the landing. During working hours, the "gig" is a motor whaleboat. Fitted with a white hood forward and flying the appropriate ensign, it becomes the "Captain's Gig" for honors and ceremony. "The enlisted man rides in a motorboat, the captain, he rides in a 'Gig.'

It don't go a god damned bit faster, but it makes the old bastard feel big..."(Sea chanty)

The Officers' Club, technically, "Commissioned Officers Mess," is a low building of unremarkable design when compared with the former royal palace housing the COM in Yokosuka. It is spacious, airy, and, thankfully, air conditioned. Against one wall is a slightly raised dais for orchestras and entertainment. The long polished wooden bar against the opposite wall is standard Navy issue in clubs around the world. Tables, some round, some rectangular, fill the space between. We choose rectangular. With Captain Stanko seated at the head, we arrange ourselves, loosely, with some regard to rank at the remaining places.

A Filipino steward's mate arrives to take orders and deliver the leather dice cup. It is time to play "horse dice" to determine whose honor it will be to buy the first round. The cup circles the table with cheers, curses, and laughter as the five dice rattle onto the table. The high poker hand of each round escapes, until only the loser remains. In some ports, losing at "horses" to eight thirsty officers could sting. In Subic, with imported beers at twenty cents and cocktails a half dollar, even the fleet ensign is not burned beyond recognition. Now the game turns to "Liar's Poker" and the stakes decline to dollars, with successive losers feeding the pot until it is sufficiently full to support the next round.

Other Wardrooms join the party, and the din expands. Voices and laughter increase in a cacophony that blends with the rattle of dice and dissonant clink of glasses. The singing begins in a succession of favorites distinct to each ship and Wardroom.

"... I can't see the target, says the bombardier, merry men are we, there's none so fair as can compare with men of the Coral Sea..."

"... It's life on these goddamn destroyers, that's making a wreck outa me..."

"... When the ice is on the rice in southern Honshu..."

"...On top of Mt. Fuji, all covered with snow..."

The sound expands beyond the club. It fills the jungle night with the sound of men. It is the sound of men who risk their lives each day at sea, exhaling.

SUBIC BAY II

Monday, 8 July 1963

Still moored starboard side to HECTOR at buoy 19. But we have company in the nest. USS COOK (APF 130) joined us in the night. A bit out of place here in Subic, as she is a command vessel for COMPHBPAC. Amphibious operations and landings. A fast transport vessel with four LCVP landing craft in topside davits. I think she generally delivers frogmen. She is basically a small destroyer with a special purpose which is not peaceful. She mounts a single 5"/38 gun forward, backed by twin 40mm cannons, and appears able to take care of herself. No crew visible topside.

John Enrud and I had the duty on Sunday and therefore felt it necessary that we stand the Monday 1600 to 1800 watch at the O Club. John is a recently arrived Ensign assigned to CHEVY's engineering department. He is from a farm in North Dakota but seems accustomed to the better things in life. Perhaps it was a large farm. His blond hair and light complexion speak of a Nordic heritage. The partial gold inlay on his upper incisor speaks of football at North Dakota State. John is one of the few bachelors on the CHEVY and might prove a suitable "steaming" companion. We are both something north of 6" and 200 lbs., so most of the local trouble should be reasonably expected to avoid us. The yin and yang of the uninitiated.

The quarterdeck of HECTOR is the departure point for liberty and shore leave transportation. Conspicuous on the quarterdeck is a bulletin board, as ordered by the Admiral. The message is a succinct warning of the various tropical diseases that might be acquired by fraternization with the local business women. The Navy is most diligent in tracking the statistical propensity to acquire such symptoms of passion in most liberty ports. In Hong Kong and Japan, where such commerce is regulated and licensed, the infection rate is under 5%. In Olongapo, the probability exceeds 90%. The statistic is punctuated by enlarged color photos of male genitalia in the final throes of infection, presumably just prior to dropping from the infected sailor's pubis like rotted fruit. It appears that even urination in a public restroom might prove hazardous. Message received.

After several San Miguel beers at the Officers' Club, we determined to test the night in Olongapo, where the only street not off limits to military personnel is Magsaysay and where it is always Saturday night when the fleet is in.

As we exit the main gate into the town, we are saluted by the Marine MP and Naval SP, posted to guard the passage and provide joint jurisdiction in the event of inter-service disputes. We cross the "Skivvy Bridge" over the "Shit River" onto Magsaysay. The river is, in fact, a highly polluted sewage canal into which local urchins dive for the pesos thrown by sailors and Marines. Clad in our tropical khaki and naiveté, we are invincible.

To cross the bridge is to step through a crack in time and onto the set of a grade "B" western movie. The town was devastated by the Spanish-American War and again by the Japanese, with a few natural disasters in between. It has gained little from restoration. The main street and only street open to the military is Magsaysay, named after the seventh president of the Philippines. Were he still alive, perhaps the street would be in better repair. But then, perhaps the street would not be named after him. It is largely unpaved and spotted with red mud potholes. The sidewalks, where they exist, are distressed boardwalks. Brightly painted "Jeepney" taxis weave in and out of the citizenry and sailors.

Barely had we crossed the Skivvy Bridge, when a form flashed from our left, banged into John, and exited into an alley, right. John stood shaking his left wrist, where moments before had been his watch on an expansion band. We were bright enough not to follow the thief into an "off-limits" alley, where his friends were undoubtedly waiting for us. So much for invincibility. We shrugged and maneuvered starboard to gain the boardwalk.

We poked around a few shops of uncertain enterprise, featuring mementos of Olongapo. There were quantities of carved monkey pod, interspersed with black velvet art memorializing the "flagellate." One proprietor proudly offered a slender carved wooden monk, which when rotated 180 degrees became a twelve-inch phallus. We declined and departed.

It was time to ingest some more attitude. Shunning the obvious fleet bars, we found a relatively quiet establishment on a second floor. If God decided to destroy Olongapo this night, it would take the waters longer to reach us.

The room was rectangular, with the requisite bar and indifferent bartender. Tables and chairs were scattered about, placed by chance or uncertain system. The patrons were no-shows, with the exception of a couple seated a few tables from us. Plantation shutters covered the windows, and large bladed fans circulated the humidity, pushing it back upon the customers. The only pieces missing were Bogart and Bacall at the bar.

We ordered "dos San Miguel, por favor," and sat back to reflect. We had each knocked back a generous gulp, when a new customer entered stage right. She was a Philippina, about the same age as the two present patrons. Her attire would suggest she was not from the local convent. She stalked directly to the seated couple. The two women entered into a spirited discussion in Tagalog, while the man nursed his beer. The timbre of the women's voices rose to the pitch of an F-8 winding its engines for its takeoff. The standing woman reached into the bosom of her peasant blouse and in a single motion produced an open switchblade. Instantly, the seated patron grasped the neck of her beer bottle and smashed off its bottom on the table's edge.

Hollywood, be ashamed. John and I had just become innocent extras in the plot of the dismal western. The two women were not into preliminaries and needed no stunt doubles. They grappled each other to the floor and rolled down the stairs and into the street, while the man ordered another San Miguel. It was time to up anchor before the local constabulary chose to arrive, should they consider this an extraordinary event. "'F' it," said John. Our tour of nighttime Olongapo complete, we headed back to the relative sanity of the O Club for a nightcap.

CARRIER OPS IN THE SOUTH CHINA SEA

11 July 1963

When we got underway this morning, SOPA was the Commander of all amphibious forces Seventh Fleet (Pacific), aboard the USS ESTES (AGC 12). Although ESTES resembles the merchantman she used to be, she is not. She is the wolf, not the sheep. Her main mast and "H" masts fore and aft bristle with electronics, like quills. She is a floating command post for the entire Seventh Fleet that does not normally spend the rainy season at this end of the earth. I understand the Marines have some lads playing in the jungles here this summer. It must be a major landing exercise to attract the senior frogman and his staff.

0945 Made contact with the USS HANCOCK, our new responsibility. The old lady should feel right at home. She saw action in the Philippine Sea during WWII and took a kamikaze hit off Okinawa in April of '45.

1031 We go to the general quarters for gunnery practice and commence firing to starboard (away from the HANCOCK). A gentle rain dapples the surface of the sea, which is calm and tepid in temperature. Away from the land, the air is cooler and fresh. I

LTCDR Campbell XO, center; CAPT Stanko, right;
LTJG Mackey, left; ducklings in white

am seated in the hatch of my Main Battery Director, surveying my portion of the South China Sea. I am lobbing 58-lb. projectiles into the briny deep with my 5' guns and spotting the splashes with binoculars. God, it is great to be at sea and a gunnery officer! We fire off fourteen rounds in less than ten minutes, which might or might not be enough to beat a kamikaze, but then, there are no more kamikazes.

The explosion of the guns is more a force than a sound. It envelopes and excludes all other awareness. The muzzles flash, the shattered air enwraps the ship and its topside inhabitants. The force of the recoil physically sets our 2250 tons of displacement sideways in the sea.

The rain runs from my battle helmet down the back of my neck. It is a pleasant sensation, a warm drip. A much more honest moisture than the humidity that saturates our existence at Subic.

I climb out of the hatch and skin down the ladder attached to the director and onto the 03 level where the lookouts are stationed. Down another level to the bridge on the 02 level. An enclosed passage ladder leads from the bridge to the main deck outside the Wardroom door. A deck below is Forward Officers, where I just have time to towel off before grabbing a quick sandwich and heading back to the bridge for the 1200 to 1600 Afternoon Watch. There is not much boredom on a warship at sea.

As I pass through, two of my new Midshipmen charges are waiting for lunch. They all arrived on board Tuesday. They are an even half dozen, and they are all mine for the next six weeks. Whatever will I do with my spare time? Perhaps work on my Counterinsurgency course? I should have their names sorted out before Midwatch. I wave and head for the bridge.

Friday, 12 July 1963, 0000-0400, midwatch

Steaming in company with TASK GROUP 77.7, conducting "local ops." A task group with that many 7s should be lucky, or at least a good poker draw. Actually, the task group consists of just three ships at this time, the carrier HANCOCK, the CHEVY, and another destroyer, USS THOMAS (DDR833). During WWII a "DDR" was a radar picket, sent well in advance of the main force. Its mission was to detect enemy activity before it reached the main body. Theoretically, this "detection" was to be achieved through utilization of its newly developed radar equipment. Practically, however, it often achieved said detection by simply being attacked.

They were a bit like the goat in a tiger hunt. Not the most envied assignment in the fleet. The CHEVY was as DDR prior to her last modernization.

Today there are no goats. Two destroyers do not provide an intimidating screen. Perhaps this portion of the South China Sea is considered sub-safe. We are just "plane guards" during flight ops and bit players in some fleet exercises.

It is raining still, some more, again. I guess that is why it is called the "rainy season." One can just imagine expatriate planters: sitting on their porches wearing baggy, crumpled linen suits, drinking too much gin, cursing the wogs and fate.

I, au contraire, cannot really curse my fate. On Tuesday last, the Midshipmen, those entering their senior year, arrived in Subic for distribution to the fleet. Each would serve six weeks on a ship of the Seventh Fleet. Numerous elements of the fleet were gathered in the bay to collect their charges. Naturally all involved mustered at the Officers' Club. A Filipino band, free drinks, and food. Subic heaven. There must have been 500 "swinging dicks," counting officers and midshipmen. To my amazement, there were about a dozen non-combatants of the Caucasian female variety acting as hostesses. They all appeared to be of drinking age, therefore probably very married to someone senior to me. Such targets represented little opportunity and a greater danger than an Olongapo debutante.

I was determined to make my midshipmen as welcome as possible here at the end of the earth. Somewhere in the Mediterranean, more fortunate midshipmen were probably attending a similar reception surrounded by French or Italian lovelies. Fortified with 86-proof courage, I formed them up in a single file. Like Father Goose, I marched my half dozen from the bar to the dance floor, quickstep. There, I selected a likely young woman, cut in on her amazed partner, and introduced myself. "I am Lt(jg) Mackey and these are my ducklings. I would be honored if you would be so kind as to dance with them."

From this point, the evening begins to cloud over in my memory. I must have made a full power run at the bar. I am not entirely clear how I arrived back on board. The next morning I awoke in my rack, fully clothed and assailed by what my roommate Ben called the RGs. "The Ree Grets." There was a note pinned to my damp chest. The note contained an address and a phone number. In a very feminine hand, it simply said "1900 tomorrow night." It was signed "Karen Karl." I had absolutely no recollection. I vaguely remembered dancing with someone. Was this someone's wife? How senior? Had she wrestled professionally? What have I done?

The day passed, assisted by the corpsman's vitamins, a handful of APC's and a mysterious pill, possibly containing a controlled substance. At 1700 I showered and changed into my "Whites." It was time to "splice the mainbrace." I had determined to go as far as the O Club and try the phone number. It took two beers to relax my dialing finger. The phone rang, and a female voice answered, "Good afternoon, Karls'." Assuming this was a surname and not a bar, I forged ahead.

"Good afternoon, ma'am, this is Lt(jg) Mackey calling for Miss (I hoped) Karen Karl."

"Just a moment please, Lieutenant, I'll get her."

A pause.

"Good afternoon, this is Karen."

The river of no return.

"This is Lieutenant Mackey; I believe we have an engagement this evening."

"Just how much do you remember, Bud?"

"Did I do anything for which I should apologize or regret?"

"I suppose you will have to take me out to dinner to find out, won't you?"

Nice voice, slightly southern.

"When should I pick you up?"

"Seven would be nice. That's 1900 hours if you are at sea. A cab will know the address. You can meet Mommy and Daddy."

Mommy and Daddy, what have I done?

At the bar, I drank some more beer and played a few games of Yahtzee for pesos with a JG from HECTOR to kill time. My bravery enhanced, I asked the bartender to call me a Jeepney and was underway.

The driver deposited me at a bungalow on the edge of the encroaching jungle. Does that make it a jungleow? A witticism to build resolve.

My knock was answered by a full captain, four gold stripes. My guess was that the "chickens" on his collar were a message to any junior officer who presumed to date his daughter. This was "Daddy," Commanding Officer of the Subic Bay Ship Repair Facility and oft times Senior Office Afloat. I was suitably intimidated, as intended.

But then, there was Karen. A beautifully rounded petite brunette. A sailor's dream. A Kappa at the University of Florida, at home for the rainy season.

Bingo, Jackpot, Yahtzee!

To be continued...

0400 The sky is overcast, the sea flat, as the Taskforce sleeps.

The rain continues.

But the rain at sea is different from that of the land.

The sea is clean, It does not rot or mold.

The rain falls to the sea and returns to the heavens to fall again.

The rain renews and refreshes the surface.

As its denizens slip silently beneath.

REFLECTION

31 July 1963, somewhere in the South Sea

The triple seven Task Force is now HANCOCK and a screen of four destroyers. For most of July, we have prowled the waters west of the Philippines from the Luzon Straits to Mindaneo, with a few days respite in Subic. Across the water to the north, Hong Kong. To the south, Saigon. We replenish, refuel, launch and recover aircraft, all with little obvious purpose.

South of the Tropic of Cancer. Sirius, the Dog Star, is ascendant. We ply the waters of the Horse Latitudes. Dog days in the Horse Latitudes. I don't know if I need an astrologer or veterinarian?

I must need something. Back in Subic, the humidity reaches the temperature. All is dampness and sweat. Clothes wilt, men wilt. My rack in Forward Officers is always damp, as the blowers rearrange the humidity. The sky spews, sucks back its burden, and repeatedly regurges.

Out here, it is better. A sea breeze and cooler temperatures. But still the feeling of frustration and longing. A need to communicate something that eludes me.

Perhaps I am just exhaling, catching up with myself? The last two years have been focused on the Navy. Surviving OCS.

Becoming a competent officer. What of the rest of my life? Time to think deep thoughts of God, man, of my future.

And still I am bewitched by the magic of the sea.
The fantasy of the days with
Water dervish dancing on
The surface
Or the nights with
Silver ripples swaying
To the magic of the moon
The stars scatter on the ebony surface
Fluorescent jelly bursts in our wake.

And then there is Karen. The women in my life most recently are not the sort one brings home to mother. Karen is a breath of the States. In a month, she will be back in Florida, and I will be chasing carriers at the end of the earth. We have no chance, but I am a little in love.

HONG KONG

02 August 1963

The Pearl River writhes from the interior of China, through the Tropic of Cancer, to empty into the South China Sea. In its estuary, Hong Kong dangles from the dragon's throat like a jade pendant.

In the gray dawn, we on the bridge are staring through the mists at a most hostile coastline. While the mountain's terrain might conceal any number of dragons, we are confronted by a more imminent and tangible threat. Our sensors detect hostile fire-control radar probing our presence. The malevolent electronic fingers detect and grasp us. They are "locked on," and their guns are prepared to fire. We are at their mercy.

China and the U.S. are no longer active combatants; however, the Korean "Conflict" is neither distant nor truly resolved. We still stand watch on the Korean DMZ. But for our revised orders, CHEVALIER would be on patrol in the Formosa Straits between Taiwan and mainland China. Suddenly we are no longer boys playing at war, but men facing the reality of mortal enmity.

And then, it is over. The fire-control radars are silent, their messages sent. We will not duel this day.

We form a column, as ordered. CHEVALIER is in the van, the hulk of HANCOCK is immediately astern. The sea is flat as the sun breaches the horizon to port. The Ngai Ying light to starboard and the Hakkok Tau light to port still twinkle faintly in the breaking dawn. The morning breeze is fresh and warm but carries a faint scent of decay.

As we enter the access to the harbor, we are surrounded by a carnival of small craft that populate its waters, darting in and out of our way like spastic minnows.

0805 Moored to Buoy 29, Hong Kong Harbor. Or perhaps "Harbour," as we are in a British Crown Colony. Our sister ships are scattered at anchor about us. We swing from a single anchor chain attached to the buoy, subject to the whims of wind and tide.

On the current tide, CHEVALIER faces northeast in the roads of Victoria Harbour. To port is Hong Kong Island, with its landings and commercial district clustered along the water's edge. Behind the shore, the island rises abruptly in a mountainous ridge, crowned by Victoria Peak. The massif commands the scene and hulks above the city as it dwarfs the offending buildings scattered below. So it appeared as it scowled down upon the pirates and merchants of the opium trade who dared its slopes two hundred years ago. So it remains, as if disdaining to be possessed by any mortal. To starboard are Kowloon and the New Territories. Both possessions were bludgeoned by the British from China in settlement of the Opium Wars.

A thousand yards beyond our bow, the Kowloon Ferry transits the harbor connecting Tsim Sha Tsui in Kowloon with Hong Kong Island, as it has since 1888. In the colony, water is the only bridge.

The harbor is alive with watercraft and commerce. Ancient junks, high-sterned with square sails, lumber among the lesser bum boats and walla wallas. Water taxis cluster to the arriving men-of-war, barely standing off, while the bum boats edge closer to hawk their wares or merely gawk.

As we rig and lower our accommodation ladder aft to port, the gaggle parts for one of the small craft. A lone figure sculls at the craft's stern, a diminutive figure stands erect in the bow, pointing the oarsman toward CHEVALIER. Chief Sager and I observe from the quarterdeck at the head of the ladder.

The craft settles alongside the platform, as neatly as a gull on a buoy. The first sighting of the passenger is the appearance of a round, lacquered straw hat rising above the deck. Immediately beneath the brim are bright, smiling eyes and a weathered Chinese countenance. She is clad in the traditional "black pajamas." Her tiny bare feet show no signs of having been bound in the barbaric tradition. The entire package, conical hat included, stands less than five feet. This is the legendary Mary Soo, one of the wealthiest citizens of Hong Kong. She is here to paint our ship. Remaining in her craft is Ah Lin, number two lady in her organization.

The chief has had prior dealings with Mary Soo, so I stand slightly aside while the deal is struck. I do not know the details, and it is probably safer if I do not. The military is not allowed to pay foreign nationals for services rendered. The bulk of the price will be paid in uneaten meals and garbage from our mess deck. The remains of the day will be carefully sorted from trays by Mary Soo's girls at the end of the chow line. The "garbage" will be canned and sold to local inhabitants. The uneaten meals will appear on the menus of Hong Kong restaurants, such as Mary's "Golden Dragon." Some liberty-happy sailors may end up paying in Hong Kong Dollars for the meal they might have eaten for free aboard.

The balance of our price will be paid in barter, known as "cumshaw." Ammunition and brass are non-negotiable, as they might be used against our own. Most likely, the chief will have to find some "useless" nylon line or coffee (known as grounds) to seal the deal.

The deal is done, and Mary Soo's ladies will paint our ship when we return to Hong Kong as "Station Ship." We supply the paint, she the labor. Her gang of ladies in black pajamas and conical hats will attack CHEVALIER from their small boats to chip and paint us to respectability.

Mary Soo is as elusive as the East and the source of sea stories. A sea story is ever a combination of fact and fancy. That is Mary Soo. She calls the girls "her children." Rumor has it that they are adopted orphans. Unwanted female children, saved from virtual slavery in a society that counts females as chattel. The price of a rural female is reported to be thirty dollars. This I believe, at least in part, as it is about the same as the price of a "hit" on one's enemy. In Hong Kong, be careful who you anger.

Mary supports and educates her children to adulthood, when they may choose to stay or leave. I like this thought. I understand that she sometimes hosts parties for her larger clients. There her daughters, like Chinese Cinderellas, appear coiffed and clad in silk to mingle with the guests. I like this fairy tale as well. But who truly knows? I don't even know if the woman before me is "the" Mary Soo. Her legend begins earlier in the century, before the war. Could this be her "daughter?" Perhaps other Marys are dickering on other ships with other First Lieutenants? What do I know? I like the story as I tell it and choose to make it mine.

At sea, we work as a unit. We man our duty stations and battle stations as a team. In port, enlisted take "liberty," and officers take "shore leave." The gulf between rank and rate widens on the "beach." The logic of this separation is both military and practical. Each group wants to experience port on its own terms, free from the formalities and sometimes animosities that separate rate and rank. Avoiding Captain's Mast and Court Martial is desirable.

At liberty call, streams of white hats flow from each respective anchorage to water taxis. The taxis disgorge their fares at Fenwick Pier, and the flow becomes a flood. Barely pausing at the pier, the flood gains momentum as it flows to the China Fleet Club. The club has been a famous refuge to the British common sailor since the late nineteenth century. The mob falls into formation along the bar, sorting itself into clumps by ship and friendship. Buying grog at bargain prices.

After a sufficient ingestion of bargain alcohol, "R & R" becomes a search for "B & B"—Babes and Booze. The China Fleet Club, by no coincidence, abuts Wan Chai, both sailors' dream and nightmare. Perhaps the roughest port of call in this part of the Pacific.

But Wan Chai has been many things in its time. During WWII, its buildings served as prisons for the inhabitants under Japanese occupation. Yet it endures. Dusk comes to Wan Chai as it did before the time of man. The sun sinks behind Victoria Peak into the vastness of the mainland. Dusk is an opiate that cools the drought and dulls the edges of poverty. The night air assimilates a thousand scents and sounds that seduce the senses. To the old, an opiate, but to the young an aphrodisiac that draws them forth into the night.

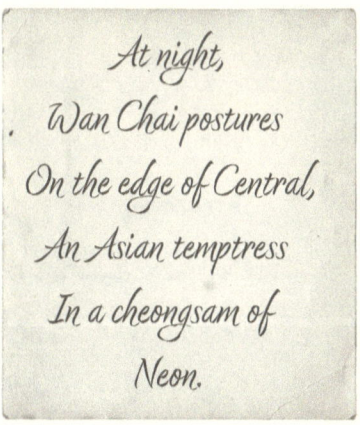

At night,
Wan Chai postures
On the edge of Central,
An Asian temptress
In a cheongsam of
Neon.

Friday, 9 August 1963

0737 Underway, steering various courses and speeds, standing out of Hong Kong harbor. Visibility is spotty. We turn our running lights off and on as we proceed in and out of fog banks. The harbor is scattered with the usual small craft skating the surface like Jesus bugs. Chinese superstition adds an excitement to this transit. Each craft believes that life attaches an ever lengthening chain of demons to its stern, like the tail of a kite. If they can pass closely under our bow, we will cut their trailing demon chain and add it to our own. Demon dodge ball.

Doug Biddle asserts that the Chinese have an additional plus to this ploy. Should they pass a bit too close and we hit them, we inherit their devils and Uncle Sam buys them a new boat. Joss.

Cross Half Moon Bay,
Ahead she steams,
The ancient junk,
With chain of devils
Streaming from her stern.
Malevolent maneuvers
Bring her close,
Beneath my bow,
Joss tormented devils
To unleash upon my brow.

HONG KONG REPRISE

10 August 1963, 0400-0800 morning watch, en route to Manila, P.I. with the triple seven task force. Time to reflect and ruminate.

Saturday at sea, and probably a long day for this sailor. Following this watch, we will refuel and then plane guard for the rest of the day.

Still catching up on sleep following a full week in Hong Kong. I have traveled some hard miles and consumed my share of spirits. I have seen sights and created scenes. I have been mobbed, robbed, and solicited. I have wandered where I should not. I have generally comported myself as a sailor on liberty and at liberty. But, I have made muster, stood my watch, and done my duty.

The "duty" part took several forms. From 1330 on Friday afternoon to 0200 Saturday morning, I was the Senior Shore Patrol Officer in Wan Chai, one of the least civilized liberty stops in the Pacific. Fortunately, I was supported by a seasoned Petty Officer and two able bodied seamen. For twelve hours, we four represented military law and order in one of the world's most colorful "combat zones."

Street level in Wan Chai is neon-fronted bars with tattoo parlors and small businesses interspersed. Half a dozen stories above, the rooftops represent a lawless subculture. In Hong Kong, every available space is utilized by its overcrowded inhabitants. The denizens of the heights are purveyors of vice and crime, drug peddlers, unlicensed tattoo artists, and diseased prostitutes. The rooftops are so crime-ridden that even the elite colony police tend to avoid them. Sandwiched between Sodom above and Gomorrah below are several laundry-draped stories of family tenant dwellings.

Less than twenty years ago, Wan Chai was a de facto Japanese prison camp, a ruin of human degradation and atrocity. But Wan Chai survives in its latest iteration. The nighttime culture is banal. Alive with neon eroticism. The buildings declare their commercial intent with illuminated signs in English and vertical banners in Chinese characters. The streets are crowded. Sailors from men-of-war and merchantmen jostle among the local inhabitants.

The bars, though many, are of single intent. To attract, to entertain, and to separate the sailor from his pay. One famous establishment is the Tenuche Hotel, where William Shatner wooed Nancy Kwan in *The World of Susie Wong*. In the bar below, cheongsam-clad bar girls dance with sailors to a jukebox and hustle watered drinks. Above, the girls entertain in other ways in rooms rented by the hour.

Liberty knows no nationality or navy. For sailors on the beach, every night is Saturday, and there is no tomorrow. It is Wan Chai, and it is all ours. We four are appointed to keep the peace. One armed officer and three enlisted men with helmets and batons against the night. The night in memory and in fact is blurred. It is in and out of bars barely distinguishable from Nom Kok. Only the patrons are varied. Some bars are the marked territory of a ship or crew. Some are marked by color or nationality. Trespassers beware. Someone call the SPs.

So we proceed, our routine established by the experience of our predecessors. The three sturdy enlisted men precede me into each bar, clad in helmets with night sticks extended. I am no coward, but the logic is faultless. The first man through the door is likely to be met with a fist. The penalty for assaulting an officer is to be avoided, and I am allowed to keep most of my teeth. By the night's end, I have been offered drinks by most of the mamasans in Wan Chai and free affection by many of the ladies. All in jest, as they know I am on duty. However we may be viewed by the sailors, we are welcomed by the mamasans. We keep the peace. Most sailors head back to their ships or the China Fleet Club. Some climb the stairs with their Susie Wongs. All must be settled somewhere before the curfew. For the Shore Patrol, it is back to the CHEVY for a short night and an early muster.

But even with the short night, by dusk, the urge to mingle and explore the night found me sitting in a walla walla with fellow officers. The boatman delivers us to "Old Blake's" pier, some miles upstream from the Fenwick Pier and a world away from Wan Chai. It is also known as "Royal Pier," since in 1899 it was originally constructed as a landing for new governors, VIPs, and royalty. This is the heart of British control and domination. Government buildings. A few hundred yards ahead, the darkened Admiralty Building surveys our landing with unblinking eyes and the arriving junior officers with no small degree of hauteur.

Still in Central, a short cab ride delivers us to Jack Condor's Bar. The proprietor is a large fisted, former Shanghai cop. Captured by the Japanese in 1941, he escaped and walked all the way to Chungking, sleeping by day in graveyards, protected by the ghosts. While not the traditional British "men's club," no women are welcome. Jack feels that men should be allowed to drink alone. Hemingway would love this bar, with ships' badges and trophies scattered about for decor. Above the bar is a stuffed alligator ridden by an iguana as a jockey. I am told it is a watering place for press correspondents.

The liquor flows, the smoke thickens, the din rises. Glasses clink, dice rattle, blending with jokes and muttered curses into a cacophony of men at play. I seem to remember that at some point, I found my way to a microphone. Besotted with brandy and bonhomie, I felt some Kipling would be appropriate. The patrons were polite, as one drunk might be to another. There was no outcry for an encore. It was time to forsake Central for Wan Chai.

The Pearl River continues to meander through Guangdong Province, as it has for eons, cutting its course ever more deeply into the earth's crust. As it passes Macau, its effluent flows into Fragrant Harbor, mingling its contents with the bilge of Hong Kong.

As the river flows southward, so do the refugees. They flow through the Bamboo Curtain of Red China as irresistibly as the river. Unlike the river, they cannot dissipate into the sea. They flood the colony with the revolution's disenchanted and dispossessed. Those who cannot find shelter in the New Territories fill the nooks and crannies of Hong Kong Island. Their settlements of scavenged wood and tin cling to hillsides unfit for goats. They live their lives on the 100,000 sampans of Aberdeen Harbor or in the closet-sized "family" units of modern highrise slums. Some spill onto the sidewalks and into the alleys.

Hong Kong, British Crown Colony. In WWII the Imperial Japanese spilled blood in Manchuria, raped China, and spread the stain of war over the map of the Far East. The "Greater East Asia Co-prosperity Sphere" lasted fifteen years. A relatively fast rape from a historic perspective. The stain of war. But then there is the slow, inexorable rape of Colonialism, of empire. "The sun never sets on the British Empire." So it must seem to those exploited. The Brits have ruled Hong Kong and the New Territories for over one hundred years. Since the Opium Wars. Their dominion will continue until at least 1999 by "treaty."

The Brits live well and rule. The people survive and subsist.

REFLECTIONS IN THE
SOUTH CHINA SEA

15 August 1963

Back at sea, free from the decay of the land. Here the presence of man makes little impression on the deep. Sea air is fresh. It has no discernible odor. The sea buries its dead, or washes it ashore to be smelt and dealt with by man.

Our chart shows us in the South China Sea looking toward Southeast Asia. According to CIC, we are 13 degrees north of the equator and just about opposite the city of Da Nang, in the country of South Vietnam. On the chart, the Vietnams cling to the lower abdomen of Southeast Asia like a section of large intestine, beginning with Hanoi in the North and descending to Saigon at the very southern tip. Directly attached inland are lesser organs of Cambodia and Laos. The question being, "What is the Seventh Fleet doing here?" I guess the obvious answer is, "Just practicing." But for what?

We have refueled, replenished, and been the sacrificial radar picket in the anti-aircraft exercise. Recently, we have been joined by the USS ROCK (AGSS 274), a fleet sub left from Captain Stanko's days in WWII. She is an old and much decorated lady who survived that war. Our prospective enemies have no ability to attack us with any weapon so ancient. But who will be next?

Whoever or whatever, we are actively playing Anti-Submarine Warfare games. We steer a zigzag course to disrupt the firing solutions of enemy subs. A tactic sometimes useful during the last war. In those days, torpedoes were fired in spreads, like bullets from a rifle. The modern torpedo seeks and homes. When fired, it first circles to detect the target, and then locks on electronically and chases down its target like a hound on a stag.

But the best part of modern ASW is SONAR. Sound Navigation and Ranging. Using low frequency sound impulses to detect objects within the basin of the sea. Technically, SONAR helps one locate and destroy an enemy sub. But there are many more interesting subjects to locate and understand in the waters beneath the waves of our world. Beneath our keel lies an entire land unexplored. A land of mountains unclimbed and great rivers uncharted. The exotic flora teem with strange and wondrous creatures. Man may walk the surface of the moon before he reaches the deepest caverns of our own planet.

While Captain Nemo needed only to step into the bridge of NAUTILUS to view the wonder of the deep, great pressures below the surface make glass a fantasy of fiction. We are privileged to be able to explore the depths through the miracle of sound. One need only pay a visit to the SONAR room. Buried in the forward bowels of CHEVALIER, it is our stethoscope of the sea. I slip into a seat and place the headphones over my ears. I close my eyes and am surrounded by the sea itself. The symphony of the sea. Whales sing songs to woo and soothe. These songs are strands of eerie notes. They begin with a sigh, rise to a wail, and end with a deeper groan. The dolphin whistle, chirp, and click. Below it all, thousands of shrimp snap and crackle in the sand. All in a world without war.

MANILA BAY

Saturday, 17 August 1963

O*600* Maneuvering at various courses and speeds to enter Manila Bay. At this hour, the world is a comfortable humid with a light sea breeze from our stern. The water surface is a hot bath. The morning sun is low, illuming the jungle and hills of Corregidor Island to starboard as the bulk of the Bataan Peninsula slides by to port. We proceed to our anchorage. Low sunbeams outline the mastheads of the scuttled Japanese fleet. The hulls mingle with other hulks of American and Spanish origin. Dead reeds in a marsh.

1 May 1898: "You may fire when you are ready, Gridley," ordered Commodore Perry. And so they did. Six United States men-of-war sank the entire Spanish fleet in a matter of hours. Captain Gridley himself was the only American casualty of that battle. The heat and stress of the battle ruined his already compromised body, and he expired a month beyond his victory.

And yet here they lie, together, the detritus of Spanish and American Colonialism commingled with the dead of Japanese Imperialism. But the dead know no flag or nation. They sleep as one in a ghostly brotherhood.

0910 We are moored portside to the USS MCKEAN (DDR 784) at Anchorage Six in Manila Bay. The news is good. While the Task Group will spend the weekend in Manila Bay, this sailor will be traveling to Subic to visit Miss Karl. Apparently there is yet some romance in the XO (a Naval Academy classmate of CAPT Karl). I have been granted two days "Basket Leave" in return for a signed affidavit releasing the USN of liability in the event that I am captured by HUK guerillas or Barbary Pirates.

Two days Basket Leave papers in my pocket and dressed in civvies. Water taxi to the pier and a cab to the Victory Liner bus terminal. Manila is the modern city of the Philippines, and yet, not. The prosperity of the west has not accrued to this former colonial possession. The crowds are a jumble of business and peasants. The clothing is loose and tropical, with straw and cotton abundant. The barong dress shirt, similar to the Hawaiian aloha shirt, was popularized by President Magsaysay and remains a favored garment even beyond his death.

As the seagull flies, Subic is one hundred kilometers away. Unfortunately, a bus is forced to travel north and west around Manila Bay and then weave between the mountains. The Victory Liner bus itself looks "prewar." I ask myself, "Which war?" Its paint is two-tone. Beige and rust. I ask myself, "Will this bus make it to Subic?" I answer, "Get on."

The riders appear to be part of the workforce returning to their respective villages for the weekend. Armed with a round trip ticket, I find a vacancy next to a middle-aged Philippine, clad in short sleeves and cotton slacks. Human engineering was not an issue when these vehicles were designed. At least I am on an aisle… briefly. Evidently the seats were designed for three, not two, and I am urged to the center by a late arrival. Two late arrivals, actually. The man is carrying a caged rooster, whose tail feathers droop upon my lap. Are fighting cocks busbroken?

We clear the city and find ourselves on two-lane pavement through a crack in time. We are on a plain of grasses edged with palms. Beyond the palms, dense jungle climbs the approach to modest mountains. At times, we have audiences of roadside urchins clad in ragged shorts and t-shirts or nothing at all. Further along, a small wooden wheeled farm cart transports a rack of hay. The smiling driver, clad in patched jeans and a small straw hat, sits astride the grim-visaged water buffalo that pulls the cart. A slender, barefooted young woman clad in a loose fitting brown cotton dress walks the roadside with a basket of washing balanced on her head.

The visible dwellings are of thatch and raised stilts. The reason for the stilts becomes obvious as we pass low-lying areas of standing water. It is typhoon season. The storms that toss us at sea wreak their own special havoc on this green land. The fact that the road is missing in places does not daunt our driver. He simply diverts to the field and bounces along cross country until the road sees fit to resume.

The rooster was evidently on a fight card near Manila and has departed without incident. My traveling companion is some manner of civil engineer during the week, but lives in a village near Subic. There he is the mayor and owns the local bar. There is no proper sidewalk, and the street is mainly clay. My friend speaks to the driver, who nods and waits. In a few minutes, he reappears with four cold bottles of San Miguel beer...enough, he assures me, to see me through the last ten kilometers to Olongapo.

Once in Olongapo, glowing with bonhomie and San Miguel, I hail a Jeepney to the jungle. It is dusk, and the interior lights illuminate the vision that is Karen, standing in the doorway. Such temptation is why Odysseus lashed his sailors to the mast. Karen hands me a cold martini, kisses me on the cheek, and whispers three words in my ear.

"CHEVALIER IS LEAVING." It transpires that our orders have changed. The CHEVY weighs anchor at noon tomorrow, with or without one LTJG Mackey. I have been the subject of an all points alert, almost immediately upon my departure this morning. I am a wanted man, and my basket leave is trash.

I take one look at Karen, the quintessential Kappa, and reflect. Using the faculties developed as a destroyer conning officer, I assess the available data and extract a plan. Upon consultation of the Victory Liner schedule, I determine that the last bus to Manila leaves at 2400 hours. That would give me approximately four hours to buy Karen a steak at the O Club and become sufficiently anesthetized to endure a return trip on the Victory Liner to Manila.

At approximately 2345 I report to the base guard shack. I inform the Officer of the Day, "I am the LTJG Mackey whom you seek. Get me back to my ship." I may well be the only sailor ever escorted INTO Olongapo by the Shore Patrol after curfew. Not truly appreciating WHO I AM, and with little deference to my rank, the SPs unceremoniously dump me into the back of the bus. My lights go out. REWIND: Victory Liner to Manila. Taxi to water taxi. CHEVALIER. Hung over, but home.

REFLECTIONS IN TRANSIT FROM MANILA TO HONG KONG

Monday, 19 August 1963

2000–2400 Steaming independently, in transit from Manila to Hong Kong. The night is clear and the sea is as calm as it ever becomes. From horizon to horizon, the heavens stare and twinkle upon our course and our insignificance. The Dog Days in the Horse Latitudes are not unpleasant on such evenings.

I'm not sure what prompted our rapid exit from Manila Bay. The rest of the task group may be off on some vital errand. As for the CHEVY, we are blissfully steaming independently to assume our duties as Station Ship Hong Kong for the next 30 days. Free from flight operations, underway replenishments and war games.

Remarkably, though somewhat unwell, I was able to make Officer's Call at 0800 yesterday. Fortunately, I was well ahead of our 1200 departure and any unpleasantness associated thereto. By my 1800-2000 bridge watch I was sufficiently recovered to do no harm. Sadly, Alfaro, a Second Class Storekeeper, was not at muster and AWOL.

Saturday night I bade farewell to Karen, before turning myself over to the Shore Patrol. She will be entering her senior year in college before I would have any chance of returning to Subic. We may not meet again in this lifetime, but it has been lovely to know her. She is the sort of person who brings to mind thoughts of marriage and family. It is difficult to fathom, but my commitment to the Navy will be satisfied in little more than a year. I have no idea what I might do with my life thereafter.

For the next 30 days, however, my future is clear and bright. I will be detached from CHEVALIER for Temporary Additional Duty as Kai Tak International Airport Liaison Officer. I will be given a temporary subsistence allowance and accommodations in a hotel room in downtown Kowloon. Each day, I will be in the office at Kai Tak, in charge of…? To be determined.

STATION SHIP
HONG KONG, BCC

Tuesday, 20 August 1963

Above Central and the Admiralty, the funicular climbs to Victoria Peak. One car ascends, propelled upward by the weight of its twin's descent to the lower station. And so they continue, as they have since 1888, a gigantic set of wall weights on a pulley. The Peak Tram was the key to habitation on the summit. Earlier inhabitants could only attain the heights by coolie and sedan chair. Colonial officials and Peak residents took "First Class" in the new conveyance. British soldiers and Colony Police were relegated to "Second Class," surely no surprise to a "Tommy." At the very back in "Third Class" would be found the Chinese and domestic animals. Little has changed in the colony.

The Summit boasts the most temperate climate in the Colony and the most enfranchised residents. From this peak, one may view the panorama of Hong Kong Island, looking northward. The crevasse between wealth and poverty is blurred by distance. Beyond the harbor, on the mainland, are the buildings of Kowloon and the fields of the New Territories. On the horizon, invisible yet omnipresent, hangs the Bamboo Curtain and the massive presence of Red China.

While the steepness of the peak limits habitation, the lower slope is densely occupied, with the buildings of Central and the Admiralty clustered about the shore. One sees the Star Ferry terminal and Victoria Harbor as in a picture book. The broad blue harbor spreads from Hong Kong Island to Kowloon with men-of-war, merchantmen, junks, walla wallas, and sampans at anchor or in transit upon its breast. From this height, the ferry seems like a toy, as it crosses the water to the Tsim Sha Tsui Terminal. Once moored, it disgorges its passengers in a wriggling knot of humanity onto the pier beneath the Clock Tower. This day, I emerge from the knot, LTJG Mackey, detached for temporary duty.

A short cab ride delivers me to the door of the International Hotel on Cameron Road in downtown Kowloon. Here I am registered with singular respect, as I am one in a long line of functionaries subsidized by the US Government. For the next four weeks, I will be a designated military representative of the United States in Hong Kong, BCC. I will be a citizen of Hong Kong. The Senior Officer Present Ashore at Kai Tak. I will be spending the eighth month on the eighth floor of this hotel. Eight is a propitious sign in Chinese numerology. It bodes well.

Arriving on the eighth floor, I am greeted by the "Floor Boy." It is he who will attend to my needs. Upon showing me to my room, he hands me a bucket. This, he explains, I must fill each evening between 7:00 and 7:30 PM, the only time during which the guest rooms have water. For drinking, there is bottled water, or distilled spirits when appropriate. This beneficence is available only in the fine hotels. Ordinary citizens queue endlessly at distribution points throughout the city for their ration. Ironically, should I miss my window, I might be forced to return to CHEVALIER for a destroyer shower and shave. CHEVY makes her own water from the harbor.

It is time to seek nourishment and perhaps a libation. While the days belong to the US Navy, the nights are mine.

KAI TAK INTERNATIONAL AIRPORT

Wednesday, 21 August 1963

0630 I arise to a cold shave, sponge bath from my bucket, and BBC Hong Kong. This is the first broadcast news I have heard since leaving San Diego in May. President Sukarno is having problems in his newly independent Indonesia. Weather, cricket scores, and the results of the races at Happy Valley. Not quite *1984*, but all the news the government would have heard. And I have a neighbor. He lives on the rooftop about a story below me and next door. He is clad in what appears to be undershorts and a torn tee shirt. His hut is a hovel, abutted by a potted garden of corn and squash. The only other residents are a mongrel bitch, her pup, and a goat. Where does he get his water?

0745 I arrive at Kai Tak. An unfortunate dabble in land development by Sir Ho Kai and son-in-law Mr. Au Tak, who created an open space adjacent to Kowloon Bay. In return for the financial disaster, the two have been memorialized in nomenclature.

The space became home to a flying school, which by 1935 had evolved into a modest airport with a hangar and control tower. In 1941, under Japanese occupation, the airfield became a prison for allied troops who were encouraged to improve the facility. To ensure a stimulating internment, they were required to convert the ancient Kowloon City Wall and the Sung Wong Yoi Memorial Tower into a foundation for a new runway.

By 1963 a modern terminal had been constructed on the site of Sir Kai and Mr. Tak's folly. It is situated at the head of the only runway, which extends some 2800 perilous yards into Kowloon Bay. The approach from the southeast to the northwest brings a pilot over the harbor and the buildings of Kowloon City. He must then descend while executing a 47-degree turn to align with the runway bordered on both sides by the waters of the bay. It is a carrier landing without the benefit of arresting wire. Welcome to one of the most dangerous landings in the civilian world. Runway number 13. All landings are visual, so the airport closes at dusk and in bad weather.

I am deposited at the curb, courtesy of a car and driver provided by my hotel. Tropical White, long trousers and short-sleeved white shirt, is the uniform of the day. Proper uniform insignia attached and white cover on my officer's hat. My predecessor has moved on, so there is none to relieve. I am met by "Mack," a representative of the American Consulate located in the Admiralty. Mack is a short, potbellied, retired gunnery sergeant, clad in linen suit and string tie. He is a veteran of three wars. His heritage is Texan and his politics closely tied to those of the John Birch society. Mack will be my mentor in all things Colonial and will respond to civilian concerns while I will man the military.

Then Mack introduces me to my "co-workers," the ladies of Jardine Services. Due to the airport's limited size, Jardine contracts with all airlines to provide landing and hostess services. It appears I will be required to work closely with some forty ladies of varied nationality, who provide said landing services. I suppose one must do one's duty.

Jardine, it should be noted, was one of the original trading companies, whose prosperity was rooted in opium.

Though I was led to believe that I would be meeting and guiding VIPs through customs, Mack informs me that those are few and far between. The bulk of my duties will relate to the processing and problems of military personnel on leave, largely from Vietnam. He then introduces me to the customs officers with whom I will work through any problems. Being forewarned about customs, I have brought a carton of "sea store" cigarettes to distribute as calling cards. Such cigarettes, acquired at sea, are without taxes and cost about $1.00 a carton. I can afford to be generous.

The airport is alive with streams of interesting people. I merge and mingle.

Sunday, 15 September 1963

2340 LTJG E.P. Mackey reported aboard from Temporary Additional Duty. Log Entry

I make my return with twenty minutes separating me from AWOL. I return on board with a bespoke wardrobe, an empty bank account, and dozens of stories, most of which I will not relate. I have existed on an average of four hours sleep a night and consumed sufficient spirits to fill a deployment. I have had an experience that will last a lifetime. On top of all, I find I have the honor of driving this destroyer out of Hong Kong Harbor tomorrow at 0800. Someone was not looking at my orders when making out the Watch Bill…or has a warped sense of humor. Time to hit the rack.

Monday, 16 August 1963

0800 Maneuvering to clear our anchorage. I have the Conn, and we stand out smartly at sixteen knots. We are underway for Yokosuka. In our wake is Mary Soo with her armada of sampans and black pajama-clad ladies. She is sending us off with seemingly endless strings of firecrackers to ward off demons, evil spirits, and perhaps hangovers.

1330 Exercised the crew at General Quarters. Set Condition 1AA. I am back in my Main Battery Director, with my gun mounts manned and ready. It is time to shake off the lethargy and banish the cobwebs. We are back at sea and playing at war.

2000–2400 I managed an hour of sleep before the watch and should get in another six before quarters tomorrow. Much better than my average for the last month. It is ironic one must return to sea to recover from the shore. Our orders have us streaming independently to Yokosuka? More time to recover.

But what an experience. The opportunity to live as a citizen of a city most souls learn about in newspapers or history books. And a favored citizen, at that. The sailors of a Station Ship are predictable economic opportunities. Four weeks of companionship and commerce.

At Kai Tak, I was seen as a potential referrer for hotels, restaurants, merchandise, and tailors. Should I so choose, I could be the beneficiary of discounts, complements, and kickbacks. I did not so choose.

Each day I was provided a list of anticipated military arrivals. It transpired that not all arrivals were anticipated, and many failed to note that Hong Kong was on daylight savings time. But I was there until the airport closed at dusk, so, no matter.

The planes and their passengers were my purpose. Most of my charges arrived in either C-47 Dakotas or the larger C-130 Hercules Transports. Whatever the flavor, all arrived without military markings. All were required to clear customs. All, with the exception of a few chrome plated C-47s that simply landed and seemed to disappear. Mack told me that they were property of the CIA. Their pilots were purported to earn $100,000 and possess a cyanide tablet they should be prepared to swallow. I thought that was only fiction?

My charges were less glamorous, but interesting as well. Most flights came from Da Nang or Nha Trang in South Vietnam. They were all "military advisors," from several services. Many were helicopter pilots with tales of having to deliver and then force ARVN troops out of their aircraft to fight. Others had training tales. All were here to forget their less than little war. Small wonder we have the elite leadership of the amphibious forces and river patrols taking the air in Subic during the typhoon season. Regardless of service or origin, it was my duty to make sure they left all small arms and ammunition on the aircraft. Hong Kong is firearms free. Even the police carry no pistols. They are, however, feared for their skill with the 18-inch baton which they carry.

They had a variety of requests. One Air Force captain left his dress uniform in a BOQ a thousand miles away and wanted me to find it for him. However, the most common request was for companionship. They wanted to party...Mackey plus Jardine Hostesses plus hotels and bars equals "party officer." I was usually able to combine the necessary elements. Sometimes I attended, but most often left them to their own devices, until they returned to their secret war.

But what were my "devices?"

One device of the first order was to take nourishment. Here there was no Wardroom Mess or Officers' Club. After Kai Tak, I wandered the streets of Kowloon in search of a suitable supper. The most common choices were Chinese, of course, but not far behind were Russian restaurants. The revolution pushed many

Russians into exile, some of whom found refuge in Hong Kong. Both choices proved reasonable, as the Yankee dollar was worth two of the Hong Kong and traded at about 410 to one with the Japanese Yen.

For late night nourishment, there was Wan Chai. There the Shore Patrol lived in the Tenouche Hotel above the Susie Wong Bar, where the off-duty patrols and the girls hosted an endless game of seven card stud. The mamasans of Wan Chai valued the Shore Patrol, who kept the peace in their bars. In return, they took turns after closing hosting late night suppers. These affairs featured ten-course meals, complete with alcohol, served by the girls, who ate and drank as well. These suppers continued for several weeks, until LT Deeto, senior SP Officer, shut them down. Fortunately for Deeto, the SPs were not permitted side arms, and he lived in separate quarters where he could not be assassinated.

But my favorite late night meal was taken on the Kowloon side. After closing, the hostesses of the No Name Bar across from my hotel take their supper. To them I am "DaBaDoan," "One who eats." We travel by cab into off-limits districts of Chinese tenements. There the buildings rise into the night like topless trees in a war-ravaged forest. The street is alive and bustles as at noon. Young and old are about their business or recreation. The warm night enfolds us in odors tantalizing, yet pungent. I should not be here, but that does not disturb me. We are the military law in the city. Life itself is a risk.

A small man in an apron greets us at the curb, and then begins opening and arranging tables to accommodate our number. Anna orders for the group, and our host commences arranging assorted seafood on a charcoal brazier. All crustaceans are grilled in the shell, and fish are grilled head and all. To do otherwise is to tempt joss. An old woman with a young child as a shill begs, and then curses when we give her too little. While we eat, an old man with a banjo fashioned from a cigar box plays "Oh! Susanna." When we are done, Anna divides the check, and we each pay our share. She summons a cab and instructs it to take me home. She kisses me on the cheek. In her husky voice, "DaBaDoan," she chuckles, "DaBaDoan."

Thursday, 5 September 1963

1831 The CHEVY got underway…without me. Typhoon Faye was bearing down on Hong Kong. No proper seaman with a choice would weather a typhoon in a harbor where his vessel might be breached or beached. He needs sea room to maneuver. I continue to man my helm at Kai Tak as ordered.

It is 1800, and the airport is technically closed. Typhoon Faye. The spirits are restless and the gods angry. The clouds hang over Kai Tak, black curtains about to fall. The heavens scowl as a C-47 bursts from the clouds above the city like a frightened sparrow. Once clear of the mountains and downtown Kowloon, it descends steeply, fighting a brutal crosswind, clawing for the runway. The trick is to get one wheel on the runway and hope the rest of the plane will follow. Somehow the pilot manages to put the left wheel on the tarmac, but he is nearly out of runway, and the next stop is Kowloon Bay. He slides to a stop with only feet between him and the fishes. Bravo Zulu, well done, captain. You will be the last to land for at least two days. Enjoy your leave. You are not on my manifest, and the customs lads have already fled for shelter. My plan is to lash myself to a stool in the No Name Bar and ride out the storm.

But the CHEVY did return after two days. I unleashed myself from the barstool. We are now back at sea, both largely recovered and unharmed. My friend Mack did stiff me for fifty dollars. "Mr. Mackey, suh, I have encountered a difficulty. Could you let me have fifty till payday?" I should have asked "Which payday?" A charlatan in a string tie. Just like gigging frogs. I am not Mack's first or last. I suppose he considers it a consulting fee, or a life's lesson learned. I thought of leaving a note for my successor. But why should he be deprived of his lesson, or Mack of his fee?

I will miss Hong Kong. Not because it has changed physically from my first visit. It remains the last vestige of a vanishing empire. Victoria Peak will continue to look down condescendingly upon the hoi polloi, until its lease expires. The people beneath the "Peak" are the true face of the city. It is they who love, hate, seek, strive, scheme, and survive. They will endure.

I will remember Kai Tak with its runway stretching into the harbor. My mentor, Mack, and the women of Jardine. A bearded Brit named Wiles, well paid to stay away from England. The men of Vietnam, and their secret war. Drought and cold shaves from a bucket. I will miss late night meals at sidewalk restaurants with ladies of the No Name Bar. Evening rides on the Star Ferry to Central and late night walla walla trips back to Kowloon with the neon of Wan Chai at my back. The view from Victoria Peak. The floating village of Aberdeen, which did float, and the Tai Pak Restaurant, which did not float. The sunset over Repulse Bay and the gray dawn of our departure.

HONG KONG TO SASEBO VIA YOKOSUKA

Thursday, 19 September 1963, 1800-2000, steaming as before.

Today I received an "ass chewing" (a technical naval term) from one J. Deeto, Jr., LTUSN, new Weapons Officer and my department head. It transpired as we were taking on fuel from the USS MATTOPONI. We were just below the bridge, in view of the CO, XO, and a half dozen of my sailors. So much for "praise in public, censure in private." I guess John missed that class. One of my Bos'n (boatswain) Mates removed his battle helmet during the evolution, which he should not have done. John stands before me, speaking largely into my chest, as he stands about 5'6". His brows creep across his forehead like wooly caterpillars preparing for a long winter. His visage is a Slavic caricature suspended beneath a too-large helmet. I am tempted to pick him up and drop him over the side.

John reported aboard during our first stay in Hong Kong. He is another "mustang" enlisted man-turned-officer. We have several mustangs aboard who are my friends, and extremely competent. Unfortunately, John is the bearer of several large "chips" on his shoulder boards. He is distrusted by the enlisted men, whom he periodically bullies, and tolerated by his fellow officers, most of whom he regards as pampered college "pukes" (his word). His favorite word is "unsat." Now he is mine to serve. My own minor tyrant. But sometimes it is the minor tyrants who shape our destiny.

No matter, it is now 2015 and I am sequestered in Forward Officers pursuing my newest collateral duty as Counterinsurgency Officer. So far, the only dimension of said duty is a Naval War College correspondence course creatively entitled "Counterinsurgency." My instructions suggest that the "current world situation" has "induced" a need that some of our number be "adequately familiar with the field." Miraculously, I have managed to submit the first two installments from WESTPAC in a satisfactory manner. Mao's treatise on guerilla warfare is explicit and compelling. Interesting as well is the notion that the ruler of North Vietnam, Ho Chi Min, considers George Washington to be his personal hero. He would very much like to ally with the U.S. to resist Chinese Communism. I wonder if any of our leaders have become "adequately informed"?

I allot two hours to counterinsurgency and turn in. I am still recovering from shore duty. Dick Hart has the watch in CIC, so I am alone in my world, which is 390 feet long and 40 feet wide. I turn on my side and place my hand on the cool steel of the hull. The vastness of the Pacific slides past my palm, a few inches from my fingertips. Above, the planets stare unblinkingly upon the ways and wars of man. A few million years is nothing to them.

YOKOSUKA

Saturday, 21 September 1963

At 0700 this AM we entered Tokyo Bay. It is now 1500 and I have the Conn. We are leaving Yokosuka after refueling. A sudden change in OPORDERS? Goodbye, Hotsie Bath and Clover Club. According to the record, we are still under COMSEVENTHFLEET quarterly employment schedule. Did they plan this change? We are ordered to rendezvous with the USS CORAL SEA (CVA 43) and Task Group 77.6 We will be operating off the coast of Okinawa in the Philippine Sea.

Wednesday, 2 October 1963

Excluding a U-turn for lunch in Yokosuka, we have been at sea for sixteen days in company with the CORAL SEA, and busy have we been. The Admiral of the 3rd Carrier Division, COMCARDIV 3, has chosen to grace this Task Group with his presence. One more Admiral. Now we have him added to the head frogman and the king of the river patrol boats. I'm sure his presence brings great comfort to the CO as he and his staff ride the Coral Sea. But I suspect his presence is the reason we have filled the past two days with war games. Steam frenetically and carry a big stick? Basically, we do little more than cut frothy ruts in the Philippine Sea to no apparent strategic purpose. To jerk us out of Yokosuka was an act of ego, which broke the hearts of no few Japanese maidens. If I sound grouchy, I am. It has been sixteen long days and short nights with no apparent purpose. Most of my friends with whom I left San Diego are gone, transferred. And I get an egomaniac gunnery officer in exchange. I pass islands in the night and wonder who lives behind those twinkling lights. I wonder what it is like to go home?

SASEBO

Thursday, 3 October 1963
Moored starboard side to the USS WILTSIE at Berth India 8. Sasebo, Japan Home of the Japanese Maritime Self Defense Force.

NAGASAKI

Sunday, 6 October 1963

Sasebo was created as a shipyard and harbor for the Imperial Japanese Navy. It nestles among some ninety-nine smaller islands scattered about the southern tip of Kyushu.

Today, I joined a CHEVALIER-sponsored tour of Nagasaki. The city is located fifty miles from Sasebo and under two hundred from Hiroshima.

On a Sunday morning in August of 1945, at 9:01 AM the congregation of the largest Catholic Church in the Orient is gathered for mass. Fifteen hundred feet above, to achieve maximum destruction, the most devastating device of man detonates. A fireball of blinding brilliance and supernatural power. A blast followed by a firestorm of biblical proportion devastates an entire square mile of the city. Is desolation not the province of the Almighty?

Eighteen years later. It is a park. In its midst, a green marble obelisk points accusingly at the sky. A few paces away, partially hidden in a grove of trees, stands a single broken corner of the church. Atop, two battered saints still walk the wall pursuing the stony path they trod the morning of the great trespass.

All around, the grass grows green and gardens bloom. Two children fly patterned patchwork paper kites.

Ghosts remain. Spirits guard the memory of those who perished in the name of peace. They honor the unintended sacrifice.

Estimates dissemble. Hiroshima, 80,000 dead. Nagasaki, 40,000. Mainly civilians. Women, children. Were they the price of peace? The planners placed the price of invasion at 250,000 military souls. We cannot ask the dead, but those who lived vote yea.

Nagasaki Park

There is a park,
Verdant with Peace.
A simple Obelisk,
Points the place above,
A gigantic fireball once,
But now
The purest blue.
Not far aside,
A grove of pines
Shelters stone saints,
Who walk a ruined wall,
Pursuing purposes
They sought
That Sunday Morning
Of
The Great Trespass.

Nagasaki Park
October 1963

THE LONGEST WATCH

10 October 1963
0414 Wardroom

The ocean knows no nation. She has no ways or walls. God is the Creator of safe harbors, but author of rocks and shoals as well. All His creation has its own way and will. The sea is no exception. She is not always welcoming. A tempestuous lady, she has her moods. There have been scorching, windless pouts in the horse latitudes. Her rages have transformed the surface of the Philippine Sea into mountains of green water with winds that shred the waves and topple ships. Tonight we are in the South China Sea off Okinawa, and she has been merely petulant. Ten-foot waves and thirty-knot winds have been her gift to me during the last watch. Perhaps my longest watch of the cruise. CHEVY is bobbing like a drunken cork in the periphery of the latest typhoon.

The Wardroom is bathed in the eerie red glow of bulbs designed to protect night vision. We are well beyond dampened tablecloths and fiddle boxes. The chairs have been lashed around the dining table, which is bolted to the deck. Cooking and consuming are near impossible. The stewards have vanished and make no attempt to prepare regular meals. I have just raided the galley for some salami around which I wrap a slice of bread. I will hit the scuttlebutt for water. All glassware and china is stowed. Water would leap from the glass.

Just aft of the bridge in his sea cabin, Captain Stanko is sequestered. The dark circles beneath his eyes are black, as though from a fight. The fight of his life. The fight for his career. The last COD flight from the CORAL SEA brought the letter from BUPERS. No fourth stripe for his sleeve, or bird for his shoulder. His second rejection. In this man's Navy, it is two strikes and you are out. Retired.

But it is the Admiral on the CORAL SEA, playing games with his task group, who pisses me off. We are four destroyers in a concentric circular screen around the carrier. "His Arrogance" has decreed "no electronic emissions." No radar. We are blind, but for our imperfect human vision as we head west at sixteen knots. CIC is blind and windowless. No help. I can check our bearing with the pelorus compass repeater on the wing of the bridge. Range is but a guess. We pitch and roll, as the wind and ocean pelt us with large quantities of green water. It is no picnic, but at least I have an idea of each vessel's relative position. Based on Captain Stanko's seniority, I have the honor of representing him as Screen Commander, in charge of the other three destroyers. The lives of my two hundred shipmates and those on our sister ships are in my hands and on my conscience. Carriers are known as tin can openers. Should one of us pass across the bow of the Coral Sea, she could cut us in half.

Not far from where we are presently, in 1944 Admiral Bull Halsey made a mistake. He took his force into a typhoon and lost three destroyers and eight hundred men in the process. His error in judgment and seamanship resulted in three destroyers "tipping turtle," turning upside down and vanishing beneath the waves with all hands. Eight hundred men who should have survived the war died with no enemy in sight. Custer only lost three hundred men at Little Bighorn. He paid the price of his error in judgment. Months later Halsey tried to "bull" into another typhoon. He survived with broken ships and a censure, but still an Admiral and hero?

Eight hundred sailors lost at sea. A statistic. Do you know how those sailors died? They died individually, as Joe or Mitch or Sal. With families, children they had never seen and never would. Some drowned relatively rapidly, some slowly, while the compartment in which they were trapped filled with water. Those in the engine rooms knew a different fate. Their carefully tended boilers, now above them, exploded when drenched in sea water. The ships and all aboard settled to the bottom into darkness and eternal brotherhood.

0320 Then comes the command, "prepare to change course." Thank you, Admiral. This order means the screening destroyers must assume the same relative position to CORAL SEA, but on a new course. The trick is to get to that station before she changes course. The carrier is much faster than her destroyers. Should one fail to be in position before the course change, they might end out of position, trailing the task group like a stray dog. Each Combat Information Center will prepare a course and speed recommendation for their vessel to reach the new station. None will be privy to the recommendations of the sister ships. Without radar, it is impossible to know the path each ship will take to station. I alert my lookouts and bridge. We will need many eyes. As screen commander, I give the order to "Execute." The ensuing scramble is like a nautical game of musical chairs. Will we die?

0359 Course changed.

I sit, braced against a bulkhead, and take a bite of my sandwich. Porter has the watch. Good Luck, Jim. You are a good officer. You will have daylight in two hours. I will hit my rack and trust you as the others have trusted me.

Was I frightened? Of course. Only fools and idiots know no fear. Bravery is only the manner in which one reacts. I believe I was too busy trying to protect my shipmates and make proper decisions to think about any emotion at the time. The God of safe harbors was with us.

YOKOSUKA BLUES

Sunday, 27 October 1963
The Clover Club

I t is getting late. The customers are few. I sit at a table in the back with Momoko and a largely empty fifth of Jim Beam. Momoko is dealing another hand of gin rummy. She is dealing, because she is winning. She is good, and I am lethargic. It is fortunate we are only playing for yen. But she will still have a decent payday before we are done. Momoko is sad. She is in "like" with Derek. Derek is "In Hack" once again and confined to the ship. He will never see Momoko or the Clover Club again. Derek is "Naval Academy" and knows the drill. He has intentionally built a record that will ensure the USN will not be his career. His choice.

Outside, it is raining. Still, yet, again. We are nearing the end of the typhoon season, so it must be the rainy season in Japan. We left Sasebo on the 10th in time to catch the latest typhoon. Should remember the name, but they are all women, and there have been many this voyage. Carriers and typhoons. I have had enough of each for this deployment. But we are not yet done.

Though the weather discourages tourism, Jim Brink and I hired a Clover Club Hostess to act as tour guide of Tokyo yesterday. Bullet Train to the largest city in the world. Large, fast, and expensive, even in yen. Saw the Emperor's Palace, the zoo, and closed down the Ginza. The Ginza must be where neon is born; it makes Las Vegas look dim. Our guide seemed to know the Ginza well. The density of the population is incredible. Jim and our guide are about Japanese height. I turned to look in a window, and when I turned back, I had lost them. I saw only a sea of black bobbing heads. My only choice was to stand still and hope Jim looked up. He did. Caught the last train to Yokosuka and made muster.

We are supposed to be in Yokosuka for upkeep and repairs. The Admiral decided that it would be fun to have a competitive administrative inspection with another destroyer. The old prankster. So we did, and it wasn't. Just one more incentive to spend evenings at the Clover Club with a bottle of Beam.

And our last stop was WESTPAC shopping. The ship is crammed with Japanese merchandise and electronics. I personally acquired a Pachinko Machine, a form of Japanese slot machine made from salvaged metal and wood. It will be my companion in Forward Officers and then a Christmas gift for my brother, John. Not a recommended state of preparedness for a warship in a sea battle. All those gifts would become lethal fragments during a bombardment. I leave my losses and remaining yen with Momoko. I wave good night to Goro-san, goodbye to the Clover Club, and catch the last cab home.

THE LONG WAY HOME

Wednesday, 30 October 1963

Happy Halloween.

0708 We will not celebrate Halloween at the Clover Club. I wonder what those ladies wear for "Trick or Treat"? The Admiral and the CORAL SEA have vanished from Yokosuka, and so must we. Some crisis, real or imagined, has pulled us, unceremoniously and unexpectedly, from our rest. So much that we seem to be leaving a few of our number behind to catch up. As we speak "Sayonara" to the folks of the rising sun, Fuji-san still hides in the mists. Six months, and I have never seen the sacred mountain. Perhaps in some other lifetime? It is a nippy fifty degrees on the bridge, with a light breeze. We will soon know what the sea has in store. Current orders have us heading back to Subic.

We have a new lady. Another carrier, USS ORISKANY (CVA 34). To some, the "Mighty O," to us, the "Big Risk." The "Risk" is escorted by a serious pair of DLGs, the newest and largest destroyers, armed with guided missiles. USS KING (DLG 10) and USS MAHAN (DLG 11). We are somewhere in the South China Sea, but headed south and west with purpose. All four boilers and thirty knots. The Bashi Channel is a shallow passage in the Luzon

Straits. We blow through it like the Super Chief through a milk stop. Rumor has it, we are on the way to Vietnam.

Monday, 5 November 1963, somewhere in the Gulf of Tonkin

Apparently Task Group 77.5 has arrived late for the party. Someone arranged a coup d'état on 2 November. We seem to have been sniffing around this piece of cheese most of the fall. This must be the reason. The ruling Nhus have been deposed and executed. Is no Nhus good news? What are we doing here?

Here in the Gulf, the sea is gentle and the weather comfortably in the 70s. Following the ORISKANY up and down the coast, we seem to be respecting the "12 Mile Limit" but remain close. A bit like a carrier task group off Long Island Sound? No matter, four more days and we head home.

My radar scope fluoresces as the strobe reaches land. It paints the coast of Vietnam in hues of undulant green, which disappear as the search turns to sea. The only way I will ever see this country.

SAN BERNARDINO STRAITS

Monday, 11 November 1963

2*000–2400* We are steaming in company with COMCRUDESFLOT SEVEN, bless his little seagoing heart. The Commodore has evidently collected what baggage he needed in Subic, and we are headed home. We are a "Task Element," four destroyers of varied vintage. Both ships and crews show the wear of a six-month deployment. The Commodore leads the way in USS BUCHANAN (DDG14), his new guided missile armed destroyer. Spaced at thousand-yard intervals, we four are playing follow our leader as he romps through the Sibuyan Sea, south of Subic at eighteen knots. (How alliterative?) Fun, no. One thousand yards in a destroyer with no brakes is a bit tight, but that is not the best part. When God was finished, He shook the last bits of Creation from his hands into the Philippines as islands. The sea is dotted with bits of land and beacons that we dodge like bumpers in a pinball machine. We are headed for the San Bernardino Straits, one of the few gaps east into Leyte Gulf. I have the deck and the Conn.

We tied up in Subic on Saturday to collect ourselves and prepare for the next eighteen days at sea. With ten alcohol-free days
behind us and eighteen ahead, John and I were determined to
tempt fate and return to Olongapo. Imagine our chagrin when we
learned that it was Election Day and no liquor was to be served.
Apparently Manila Rum mixed with Coke and poured "under the
bar" is considered patriotic in Olongapo and not illegal. We are,
once again, actors in a bad Mexican western. The camera frames
downtown from above. The torch-lit streets and sidewalks are
crammed with shouting partisans. The candidates roll past, standing in the back of painted jeepneys. There are no bands, only the
roar of the crowd and the staccato crack of firearms. The camera
zooms in on two large Angelos clad in naval khakis. Each supported on either side by a sympathetic Olongapo business woman.
The camera fades to black. My last memory of Subic.

CHEVALIER is in station two, directly behind the Commodore
as we enter the strait, which is not particularly "straight." It is
a narrow channel ten miles long. Towering cliffs stand sentinel
on either side. The passage is rock studded and swept by capricious currents. No sea room to maneuver, if attacked. Tonight the
waters seem to boil with the restless spirits of those who have died
here over the centuries, trapped in this transit.

*25 October 1944, a short aside on an event
from nineteen years ago:*
**Admiral Kurita and his Main Battleship Force burst
from the eastern exit of the strait into Leyte Gulf.
His fleet is battered, yet lethal. This morning, the
Admiral stands on the bridge of YAMATO, the
largest battleship ever built. Behind follow three
more battleships and an assortment of cruisers and
destroyers. As he enters the gulf, he is prepared to**

face Bull Halsey and his carrier force. Bushido. The code of the Samurai. The Admiral scans the horizon for his adversary, and what does he find? Nothing. Redemption.

Halsey, obsessed as Ahab, has been suckered north by a fleet of toothless Japanese carriers. He has abandoned the strait and MacArthur's invasion fleet. What remains to blunt Kurita's charge are seven destroyers and a half dozen "Jeep Carriers" fifty miles to the south. My cousin Bob is on one of the carriers. Jeep carriers support invasions; they do not fight battleships. The 5" guns of a destroyer would merely bounce off the armor of YAMATO. All these vessels are Pawns to sacrifice in the naval game of chess.

To the south horizon CDR Ernest Evans, USN stands on the bridge, as captain of USS JOHNSTON (DD577), a newly commissioned Fletcher Class destroyer. Known by his Annapolis classmates as "The Chief" for his Cherokee heritage. He is a remarkable exception to the white elitism of the time.

The October day is gray with a marine layer hugging the choppy sea. What does Evans see? Not the "nothing" he expected, but the masts of YAMATO and the fleet, rising from the sea on the horizon like Armageddon. Then occurred one of the most remarkable feats of seamanship and courage in naval history. First, he forms the destroyers to lay down a confusing smoke screen to protect the carriers. He then orders his destroyers into sacrificial charge. All engines ahead at flank speed, dodging from shell splash to splash; he executes a torpedo attack that confuses Kurita. Incredibly surviving this charge, he rallies the remaining destroyers. Torpedoes gone, they attack a second time with 5" guns, firing only at the topside spaces where armor is light or non-existent.

His delaying action convinces Kurita that he faces a greater force and buys time for the invasion fleet to rally reinforcements. With that second charge Evans was carried to his death and into history.

We exit the Strait, as did Kurita, but file homeward across the gulf and into the Philippine Sea. Perhaps my keel is crossing Evans' bones. After JOHNSTON went down, he was never seen by any of his crew. I like to think his fighting spirit rose to sit in counsel in the longhouse where all true warriors rest. If I should die in battle, I would wish to do so from the bridge of a destroyer. With battle ensign flying from my masthead, bagpipes skirling, I order "left full rudder, engines ahead at flank speed," dodging shell splashes into conflagration and Hereafter.

Shakespeare named those who fight for common cause and live "a band of brothers." But what of those who fight and die? The dead know no nation or navy. They know no cause. They are now a brotherhood of all who dared to go to sea, willingly or not. From the first dugout canoe to the newest nuclear sub, our brotherhood reaches across oceans and ages. A typhoon knows no favorites. Japanese or American; each knows the same storm and risk. Each dies equally as dead. The brotherhood of the sea.

REVERSE

Friday, 15 November 1963
Guam, Mariana Islands Apra Harbor

The island of Guam looks like a booted foot, toe pointed toward Japan. One more volcanic jungle for which too much blood was spilled. Over 20,000 killed and 7,000 injured to rule 200 square miles of whatever flora and fauna escaped the carnage. Slightly larger than the District of Columbia. The Japanese went down six to one American. The jungle is so dense that there are probably isolated holdouts waiting to continue WWII as we refuel.

I am weary of all things martial. We are headed home. I feel as if we have been a "ship in the bottle" of WESTPAC. A jumble of seas and storms, lands and ports. Politics and manipulation driven by duty. The cork is pulled, and we are free to flow eastward into the open sea, without restraint.

We steam steadily northeast at a brisk twenty knots. The sea is moderate and the temperature a comfortable eighty degrees with light wind. Though we have no known enemies in this part of the Pacific, the Commodore seems compelled to remain martial. We, his minions, move from a "loose lines abreast" formation to a Diamond, and thence to a Column. We practice changing stations and within said formations. He must think he is back on the Severn River at the Academy drilling Plebes. And yesterday, we even went to general quarters. I really did not mind the opportunity to view the world from my hatch in the director. The sun is gentle and warming on my shoulders and neck. We fired twenty rounds of anti-personnel projectiles into the waves, no casualties, with the exception of a few surprised fish. No sea birds were harmed.

Sunday, 17 November 1963

We are officially downgraded to non-combatant task element, no longer part of the 7th Fleet in WESTPAC.

Two years ago today, I flung my Officer's Hat into the air, with the rest of my OCS classmates and received my first salute from Chief Harry. I have been officially proclaimed an "officer and a gentleman." From my first day at OCS to this Sunday in mid-Pacific, my life and mien have been changed forever. I am trained to "fight my ship," to kill and destroy when called upon to defend my nation. Circumstances did not so demand in the Gulf of Tonkin. But it was a "War Zone." My oath and duty implicit, if ordered. It was not a game.

While my peers and classmates are preparing to be doctors and lawyers, my country has entrusted me with millions of dollars of equipment and the lives of men. Whatever life brings, I will probably never again hold such responsibility. Chief Marble, I learned your lessons and have kept the faith.

Tuesday, 19 November 1963
The International Date Line

Remember 31 May, the day we lost on the way to WESTPAC? It has come back as 19 November. We now have two of them. We used the second one to refuel at Midway and head for Pearl Harbor.

RETURN TO
PEARL HARBOR II

22 November 1963

Sunrise. Maneuvering at various courses and speeds entering Pearl Harbor. We move past the rusted gun barrels of ships long dead and the empty battleship moorings, with small notice.

Guns will be of little use in this war. John Fitzgerald Kennedy, President of the United States, has been shot. What better time for the Russians to attack? A year ago, we were headed for the Panama Canal and Cuba, when the Commander in Chief faced down Khrushchev. At least there are no Russian missiles in Cuba now. But what of Vice President Johnson? JFK has treated Lyndon as an idiot child since the election. How would he face Mr. K?

We tie up at Pier 10. Commerce taking on fuel and replenishing our depleted supplies. Refuel, replenish, and get out to sea. No one wants to be stuck in Pearl Harbor if we are attacked. Stationary targets in a strategic harbor. Ducks on the pond. Typhoon or attack, the place to fight is at sea.

The harbor is a classic flap, with all ships attempting to top off and exit. I find a phone booth on the pier, but all lines to the mainland are overloaded.

1100 Underway, with the LTCDR Campbell at the Conn. The first time I have seen him take charge on the bridge. We leave the ARIZONA Monument in our wake, clear the harbor, and head southeast at twenty knots.

1200–1600 I have the Deck and Conn. We are down to three ships. TOWERS must have remained in Pearl. Our Task Unit has reformed and heads northeast at fifteen knots. Waiting for news and orders. Seventy degrees with a modest sea and stiff breeze. The mood is surreal. All is a state of numbness. When will the blow strike? Where?

But then the Commodore comes to the fore to restore our resolve. Nothing like tactical exercises to lift the spirit. We three. Back to games from the Severn River. Boys in rowboats. And then the command…in code, naturally. I have been at this long enough to recognize many orders. I do not recognize this one? That is for the watch in CIC to decipher. But they cannot find it in the code book? And then the order to "Execute!" The other vessels begin to move. I choose to maintain course and speed, as my safest option. Then the Commodore's voice over the radio. "NEGAT BRAVO ZULU, RECLAIM," for all to hear. "Badly done." Where the hell did he get that formation? More games for the "Annapolis Old Boys Club?" I am tempted to reply "FOXTROT UNIFORM," but Captain Stanko has his own problems. My cheeks burn, and I say nothing. My watch is over, and I suffer naught but a wounded professional ego. The President is still dead.

ZULU JULIET NINER

27 November 1963

1053 Buoy 1SD

We are not at war with Russia. The bell buoy still bobs and clangs as it did seven months ago. The sea is moderate, the day is clear. The browns and greens still mottle Point Loma in the distance as we approach the channel.

Since May, we have steamed...over 40,000 nautical miles...ten times around the earth. They have not been easy miles. Traveled in the van of task groups and the wake of typhoons. We have inched through black, wave-tossed nights and churned through dancing heat at thirty knots. We have patrolled, watched, guarded, and threatened. We have sweated, laughed, sworn, slept...and then risen to do the same in different order.

Zulu Juliet Niner. "Detached to proceed on duty assigned." How many times has that order set our rudder over and our engines ahead?...A new task. Another port. This time it means, "Proceed on your homeward journey." There will be no more tasks, no more ports on this cruise. Your job is done. BRAVO ZULU. Well done.

The cruise for which I traded three and a half years of my life is done. But I will remember... Lands and land. Ports and people. Storms and stills.

I will remember the clear blue, brilliant greens and rugged blacks of Hawaii on the horizon. Pearl Harbor and Battleship Row, banks cluttered with the guns of dead ships and defeat. There will be the insignificant stretch of sand called Midway and bravery that changed the course of a war. The sensuous smells of nature and humanity comingled as we entered Tokyo Bay. Sagami Wan, Osaka Wan. The Shrines of Kyoto and the dancers of Takarazuka. The pungent smell of Saki, like fermenting apples. The pusher boats of Sasebo and the obelisk of Nagasaki. Subic Bay Officers' Club, Manila Bay, the Victory Line, Olongapo, Manila rum. There will be Hong Kong, Wan Chai, and Kowloon. Kai Tak Airport, with Mack and the Ladies of Jardine. The Military Advisors of Da Nang. Mary Soo. I will view the coup from the Gulf of Tonkin. I will clear the San Bernardino Straits with the ghosts of Admiral Kurita and Captain Evans. I will remember.

But most of all, I will remember that for seven months of my life I lived...I ate, I drank, I laughed. I sweated, I swore. I watched, I thought, I felt, I joyed, I sorrowed, and I loved. But most of all, I lived with every fiber and ounce of my existence. I lived as if each moment were my last. If I can fill each moment of life as I have lived the past seven months, I will live as much of life as man may and I will not regret. Hawaii, Midway, Japan, Hong Kong, the Philippines, the Gulf of Tonkin...Sayonara.

Wednesday, 27 November 1963

Moored pier 4, U.S. Ship Repair Facility, San Diego, California. Ships present include various units of the US Pacific Fleet, foreign men-of-war and yard and district craft. SOPA is COM FIRSTFLEET in USS ST. PAUL (CA 73). E.P. Mackey, LTJG, USNR, signed Log

> *The span of Man is a grain of sand*
> *On the shore of history,*
> *But the sea rolls on from Creation's Dawn*
> *To the Dusk of Eternity*

CHEVALIER is gone. CHEVALIER is a ghost ship now. But she and her crew will sail the reaches of my mind, till I shall cease to be.

LTJG Mackey

HISTORY

Somewhere between "What Was" and "What Might Have Been" lies the perception we call "History."

The assassination of JFK is perhaps the most viewed and recorded historical event of all time. That it happened is an undisputed fact. How and why it happened will remain the perception of the individual historian and his selective interpretation of available data. Ultimately, the written or recorded word will become fact rather than the act itself.

My intent is to show something of who I was during my place in time. My framework is based on what historians consider primary documents. My mother lovingly retained most of the letters I wrote during my military service. The United States Navy has preserved the Smooth Deck Logs from her commissioned vessels in the National Archives. I can access where we were, what we were doing and with whom, hourly during my military service. While at sea, those logs recorded latitude, longitude, and weather. When I reference a time or place, the fact and perception coincide. Unless I choose to alter the perception.

For verification of historical data, I have relied primarily on Wikipedia. For the details of Leyte Gulf, I have drawn upon SEA OF THUNDER, by Evan Thomas.

The opinions, however, are entirely mine. Any respect or disrespect is purely intentional.

River of Man

"Human history is a river, flowing inexorably into the sea.
Each act of Everyman feeds another, and another...
No act, fair or foul, is without consequence.
Man can neither un–drop a bomb nor un–say a word.
Each act flows forward as a droplet of the River of Man,
To be deposited in the Ancient Womb.

Homeward bound

NAVSPEAK GLOSSARY

Airedale A naval aviator. Brave, crazy. One must be slightly deranged to want to land a jet on a carrier. Receives well deserved Flight Pay for this aberration.

Air America The CIA's air force in Vietnam. Theoretically secret. Spook pilots were reportedly paid $100,000+ and issued cyanide capsules. Certifiably crazy.

Anchors Aweigh Not "away." Report to the bridge indicating the anchor is free from the bottom and the ship is officially "underway."

Attack Carrier The bane of a destroyer man's existence. Inhabited by Airedales and sailors. About three football fields in length. Frenetic. A small war unto itself.

Aye Aye Response to an order. "I understand, I will comply."

Benjo Ditch Open pit or canal used to contain human waste for agricultural purposes. Fishing or boating is discouraged.

Bilge Lower reaches of a ship where seawater sometimes drains. Also a term for mindless gossip or senseless statements.

Bilge Out Fail to graduate from OCS. Does not terminate military obligation and results in two years active duty as an enlisted seaman.

Bird "Chicken" The eagle insignia worn on the collar of a "Full" Captain. "Full," not "Fool."

BOQ Bachelor Officers' Quarters. Way station for unmarried officers between assignments or attending schools.

Bridge Area of a ship containing the "Wheel," from which the ship is driven and controlled.

Bulkhead "Walls" of a ship.

BUPERS Bureau of Personnel. Responsible for administrative matters relating to assignment and advancement.

Captain's Mast A form of NJ P(Non Judicial Punishment) with the ship's captain presiding as judge in cases not requiring courts martial.

C-130 Heavy duty cargo plane. All purpose. Used to transport troops from Da Nang and Nha Trang to liberty in Hong Kong.

C-47 Another multipurpose workhorse. Transports smaller numbers of troops. Gunslip, Ambulance. CIA Spy Plane.

Cheongsam Clinging silk dress, slit on one side from hem to varied elevations. Not normally worn by school teachers or moms to market.

CO Commanding Officer. John Stanko. Usually refers to ship's Captain.

COD Carrier Onboard Delivery. Helicopter transfers from carrier to support ships. Mail and men.

C.O.M. Commissioned Officers' Mess.

COMPHIBRON SEVENTH FLEET Navspeak for the admiral in charge of amphibious forces of the seventh fleet. Head frogman.

Conn Refers to the watch officer designated to give orders to the helmsman.

Deck Officer in charge of the Watch has "The Deck."

Deck and Conn "I am in charge of the Watch. I will give the orders to the Helmsman. Your lives are in my hands."

DD Destroyer "Tin Can," "Small Boy," "Cowboy" to the carrier.

DDR Radar Picket Destroyer. Leads carrier groups by miles to detect enemy. Low life expectancy. Duck sitting on a pond.

Dog Days Usually the hot and humid days of August, when Sirius, the "Dog Star" is ascendant in the heavens. "Stinking hot," as my father described it.

Dog Watch The watches split into two-hour durations, 1600 to 1800 and 1800 to 2000, allowing both watches to eat supper. The split also creates a rotation in the watch schedule, allowing watch sections to move through the clock, rather than standing the same watch each day.

Engine Order Telegraph Mechanical Device manned by the helmsman sending orders to the engine room to alter speed. Activation of the handle resulted in bell tones heard by the watch.

ENO Elements of Naval Operations. A manual used to encode inter-ship communications between allied vessels. Labeled "Confidential," but probably memorized by the Russian Navy. Issued to each Officer Candidate to help teach control of classified data. A millstone and disastrous if misplaced.

Execute Order to commence an order or action. Not capital punishment.

F-4, F-8 Fighter jets, flown by Airdales from the deck of carriers.

Fiddle Box Rectangular wooden box attached to dining table to restrain tableware in tough weather. Not always effective.

Five Inch Thirty-eight 5"/38 Naval gun firing shells 5" in diameter with barrel Mk 38. Shells weighed 58 lbs. Effective range was 7 to 8 miles. CHEVY had three twin mounts, for a total of 6 barrels which could fire simultaneously upon a target.

Flap Noun. Imagine pouring a bucket of cold water on chickens. The result is an event or communication roughly similar in result.

Flank Speed Maximum speed possible. "Get me out of here."

Full Rudder Maximum rudder angle to turn the ship sharply. "Get me over there."

Gili Gily A Filipino dish made of marinated pork or chicken. Stewards would leave it in the Wardroom fridge, from which I would liberate it upon late night return from shore leave.

Gouge Noun. True inside information. Refers to test answers passed from one OC section to the next.

Gun Deck Adjective or verb. A deck on a sailing ship containing the ship's guns. As a verb, it refers to writing a report on the "Gun deck." A false or fallacious report.

Hack Non Judicial Punishment for an officer, usually confinement to the ship during in port stays.

Hatch Doorway in a ship. Every hatch has "dogs" that secure it to ensure watertight integrity during storm or battle.

Helmsman Members of the bridge watch at the ship's wheel and engine-order telegraph.

Horse latitudes Band 30 degrees north and south of the equator, known for dead calms and flat seas. In ancient times, sailors running low on water would cast any horses overboard to conserve their supply.

Hotsie Bath A spa consisting of a series of baths and showers conducted by a diminutive Japanese woman clad in white shorts and shirt. Begins in a steam cabinet and ends with a thorough massage, during which said attendant walks on one's back to loosen large muscles. Usually no monkey business, as attendants are licensed professionals in the art of massage. A destroyer man's dream after weeks at sea on limited water rations. It's the water, not the woman.

Jeep Carrier CVE's Known as "Woolworths" or "Baby Flat Tops," for diminutive size and cost compared to Attack Carriers. The US Navy could afford to lose three jeep carriers in battle at the cost of one Attack Carrier, usually used to support amphibious landings. Also used to ferry replacement aircraft to war zones. Heroes in Leyte Gulf.

Joss A combination of luck and fate. Found a lady...good joss. She has a husband...bad joss.

Knots Nautical miles per hour. A nautical mile is 2000 yards. 30 Knots is about 35 MPH.

LOI Letter of instruction. Outline detailing order of movement.

Loose Cannon In the days of sailing ships, naval guns were fitted with wheels and tied in place in gun ports. If one broke loose in a storm, it would roll frenetically about the deck, causing great damage. Someone with an unpredictable mien or mouth is known as a "loose cannon."

Mamasan In Japanese, "san" is a sign of respect. Mamasan would mean a respected mother. The title is applied to the manager or owner of a club or bar.

MPC-"Mickey Mouse Money" In 1963, when in Japan, we were paid in Military Payment Certificates, which could only be exchanged on the base for yen. The fixed rate was 360 yen to the US dollar. Dollars on the open market, which were forbidden, were about 420 to one. Looked a lot like Monopoly money.

Mustang A sailor who ascended from the enlisted ranks to commissioned officer. Usually good officers, but sometimes considered traitors by enlisted, not sure why a Chief Petty officer would want a commission.

Officer's Hat "Lid" A "billed" hat featuring the distinctive Navy Eagle insignia. The covers could be changed from khaki to white to match the appropriate uniform. For senior officers, the bill is embossed with gold leaves known as "scrambled eggs." The only occasion on which I became seasick, I quietly removed my lid and barfed in it.

One MC 1 Speaker/Public address system heard in all spaces throughout the ship.

OOD/JOOD Officer of the Deck/Junior Officer of the Deck. Officer empowered to give orders to the watch section. Responsible for maneuvering the ship. JOOD is usually OOD in training.

OPORDER Operation Order. Usually based on LOI. Sometimes it makes sense.

Overhead Ceiling of compartment.

Pisscutter "Fore and Aft" cap. Looks a bit like an overturned canoe. Made of khaki cloth. Often worn at sea as less likely to be blown off one's head. As it is pointed, tends to cut though the "piss."

Plebe Freshman at the U.S. Naval Academy. Lowest form of life.

Pork Chop Supply Officer. Supply Officers have a special designation and are not eligible for command at sea. Do not stand bridge watches at sea. Sometimes stand in port watches.

Port Hole Ship's window. Most do not open. None below the main deck on a warship.

Reclaim Call sign for the USS CHEVALIER. Used to identify source of radio communication or object of an order.

Screw Slang for propeller, not a salacious act.

Scuttlebutt On a 19th-century sailing ship, a "scuttlebutt" was a cask containing water. The "butt" was the cask, with the "scuttle," the hole cut for a dipper. Thus newer forms of acquiring a drink are "Scuttlebutts." Since the butt was a gathering place, it became the source of discontent and rumor. Not unlike the current "watercooler." Thus, "scuttlebutt" is also unsubstantiated rumor or grousing.

Severn River Body of water at the U.S. Naval Academy upon which the cadets cavorted.

Short Arm Penis.

Skivvy Boxer type underwear issued in the military. Also a slang for most types of underpants, male or female. "Ichiban skivvy honcho" – Number one man with the ladies.

SOPA Senior Officer Present Afloat. The military is a vertical organization. It is always important to know who is in charge. One can always hope they know what they are doing.

Task Force Fleet Operational Unit of the US Navy.

Typhoon A hurricane that rotates in the opposite direction. Shaped somewhat like a racetrack, with a calm "eye" in the center. Wind speeds in excess of 74 mph and mountainous waves. Identified by women's names. Capricious.

Underway The anchor is free of the bottom. All lines are clear from the pier or buoy. The ship is free to maneuver.

Way Movement or motion of the ship.

Wan Body of water. Bay, in Japanese. Not pale.

Water Hours A ship distills all water from the sea. Steam is its means of locomotion. Therefore all other usage is collateral. Water for drinking, cooking, bathing, and laundry is limited to less than 20 gallons per day per man. No long hot showers.

WESTPAC Western Pacific. Primarily Japan, Philippines, and the South China Sea.

White Hat Round white hat worn by enlisted sailors. As a noun, it refers to the sailor himself.

Word Order or instruction. "Passing the word" is forwarding an instruction or order.

XO Executive Officer. The Captain's right hand and enforcer. CDR Campbell.

Yen Japanese money, not a longing for companionship.

Zulu Juliet Niner "Released to proceed independently on duty assigned."

The end.

About the author

After graduating from Princeton University in 1961, author Edmonds "Bud" Prufrock Mackey served as an officer in the US Navy and spent most of 1963 in the Pacific aboard the USS *Chevalier* (DD 805). He is the author of *Princess of the Mockingbird, an Illustrated Fable*.